Childhood in Society

for Early Childhood Studies

Rory McDowall Clark

First published in 2010 by Learning Matters Ltd
Reprinted in 2011(twice)

British Library Cataloguing in Publication Data
A CIP record for this book is available from the British Library.

ISBN: 978 1 84445 384 9

This book is also available in the following ebook formats:
Adobe ebook ISBN: 978 184445 731 1
EPUB ebook ISBN: 978 184445 730 4
Kindle ISBN: 978 085725 006 3

Cover and text design by Code 5 Design Associates Ltd
Project management by Deer Park Productions, Tavistock, Devon
Typeset by Pantek Arts Ltd, Maidstone, Kent
Printed and bound in Great Britain by the MPG Books Group

Learning Matters Ltd
20 Cathedral Yard
Exeter EX1 1HB
Tel: 01392 215560
info@learningmatters.co.uk
www.learningmatters.co.uk

Contents

The author

Rory McDowall Clark originally trained as a nursery and primary teacher in Brighton and has wide experience in broader social contexts including community development with charities, voluntary organisations and outreach youth work. Rory worked as an educational consultant for Cheltenham Borough Council and Gloucestershire County Council before taking up a post in the Centre for Early Childhood at University of Worcester where she has been a senior lecturer for the past ten years. She has an MA in Sociology: Contemporary Studies and her research interests include gender, cultural views of the child and continuing professional development.

Acknowledgements

Every effort has been made to trace the copyright holders and to obtain their permission for the use of copyright material. The publisher and author will gladly receive any information enabling them to rectify any error or omission in subsequent editions.

Introduction

There is an old saying that my grandfather often quoted which goes 'Children should be seen and not heard'. This may well have been true at one time but is certainly not so today. In fact to a large extent one could argue that the reverse is more accurate. While we now increasingly recognise the importance of listening to children and paying attention to them, they are *seen* very little. Children do not play out in the street any more, they are rarely allowed to travel to school on their own and they are no longer sent on regular errands to the shops as was common when I was a child. Children spend an increasing proportion of their time in specially designated places such as day nurseries, out-of-school clubs and their own bedrooms, frequently fitted out with the latest technology. Childhood is progressively more regulated so that instead of being a natural part of public life, it takes place in private (Valentine, 2004). In a relatively short time expectations attached to the social category of childhood have changed radically and this has profound implications for the actual lived experience of modern day children.

In recent years children have been the focus of unprecedented attention from all quarters of society (James et al., 2001). Parents, educators, politicians, manufacturers and the media have all turned the spotlight on children and there has been a corresponding concern about the status of childhood. This increasing awareness has brought many benefits, but also a number of negative consequences for children themselves.

The higher profile of childhood is also very evident in universities and among academics and researchers. When children were regarded as primarily the concern of their mothers and their teachers, they were studied as 'units' within the family and the school system. However, an increased awareness of childhood as important in its own right, has brought a corresponding growth in the study of childhood as an academic subject. Alongside this runs a proliferation of university courses preparing people for professions working with children. The Every Child Matters agenda (DfES, 2003) has established the need for interagency working and this reinforced the move towards an integrated children's workforce incorporating increased professionalisation (McDowall Clark and Baylis, 2010). As a result, the number of courses which focus on childhood has grown significantly.

This book is intended primarily for students embarking on such courses and beginning to study childhood. You might have recently left school and just begun a degree programme or you could have considerable experience behind you and are returning to study. You will have an interest in children and a desire to work with them; you may have spent plenty of time with children or possibly very little; but it is likely that most of your thinking about children is to do with individuals and what they do. You have probably not given a lot of thought to the social institution of childhood itself and the ways in which childhood is enacted within society. This book is intended to support students and practitioners in exploring these concepts.

Everyone's ideas and attitudes to childhood are shaped by their own circumstances and memories (Gabriel, 2010) and this is a useful resource to draw on. However, it is also necessary to move beyond personal experience to *examine* these perceptions of childhood and the implications they carry. Different understandings about the nature of the child affect attitudes and behaviour towards children. Similarly, assumptions about what constitutes an appropriate childhood underlie provision and policies related to children. The intention of this book is twofold: the information it contains should support your growing knowledge of how childhood is affected by society and societal influences. However, it should also help you to rethink some of your suppositions and evaluate evidence so that you can successfully challenge ideas and assumptions where necessary and act as advocates for children and their families.

Traditionally the study of childhood has been dominated by two perspectives: the psychological and the sociological. Social explanations of childhood have by and large been based on the concept of 'socialisation', representing children as passive objects who are acted upon by influential adults so that they can develop and mature to become full members of society. Since the end of the twentieth century a rather different outlook has come to the fore, often referred to as the new social studies of childhood (Prout, 2005). This approach acknowledges the perspective of children as active participants in their own lives and seeks to place childhood within all the social studies disciplines including history, geography and anthropology.

This book focuses on a sociological approach to aspects of childhood but takes a broad perspective to bring in matters of social policy and history as well as conventional sociological factors. There is a growing number of texts which focus on these various fields; what makes this book particularly valuable is that it draws together these different topics within one place. As such it is essential reading for new undergraduates but it is also hoped that those who are more advanced in their studies will find much of interest here.

How to use this book

Although organised in a systematic manner that builds on concepts from the beginning, it is recognised that few people read academic texts in the same way they do novels – by starting at the beginning and reading consistently until they reach the end. Mostly you are likely to pick up this book and dip into it according to current interests and requirements, quite possibly skipping from one section to another to make your own links and connections. Although each chapter stands alone and can be read in isolation, there are evidently strong relationships between various aspects of the child's place within society (Bronfenbrenner, 1979). For this reason connections between different chapters are clearly signposted within the text to enable a reader to find further information and follow up issues elsewhere.

Each chapter begins with a box outlining what will be discussed within it and at the end there is a summary of the main points raised. Activities for individual reflection or group discussion should help readers to engage with ideas and apply them to real situations to develop their understanding. A number of text boxes explain concepts raised and clarify some terms while each chapter contains suggestions for further reading which are annotated to encourage study. There are also links to websites which can provide helpful background information. The timeline at the end of the book will help readers recognise the relationships between different issues raised in separate chapters.

Chapter 1 considers the recurrent predicament of childhood studies – what is childhood anyway? This seemingly simple issue is a good starting point because everything we say about children is dependent on it. The dilemmas resulting from attempts to define the social category of childhood are considered and the implications of these discussed. The chapter also presents a way to think about the child within society that recognises how wider community, national and international issues impact on children's lives. This theoretical approach, known as an ecological model (Bronfenbrenner, 1979), underpins the rest of the book.

Chapter 2 gives a brief account of historical perspectives to show how childhood has developed over time. This helps to contextualise the way social institutions surrounding childhood, such as family and school, have come about. It also identifies how many key ideas about children and childhood have arisen which continue to impact on policy and practice in the present day.

Chapter 3 examines the child within the family. There have been considerable changes in the structure of families since the Second World War and this has caused anxieties about children's first experiences within the home. This chapter evaluates those changes, examines perceptions of the breakdown of traditional families and considers some of the consequences of these concerns. Theoretical explanations and critiques of the family are presented and used to examine the ways in which the state impacts on the family.

Nowadays many children spend a large proportion of their lives within specially designed provision and Chapter 4 considers the repercussion of this for Early Years settings. Concepts such as quality and inclusion are examined as well as the background to curricular frameworks and the consequent implications for the children's workforce and partnerships.

The focus of Chapter 5 is the neighbourhood or community and the way in which this influences the experience of childhood. The impact of social exclusion on children's lives is raised and childhood is considered in relation to ideas about public space.

Chapter 6 takes a broader perspective to outline how the national context shapes children's lives and the place of children and families within social policy. The ways in which political ideology affects public welfare is examined and related to different models of social welfare. This chapter also considers the increasing differences between the four nations of the United Kingdom as a result of devolution.

Chapter 7 reflects on the global context of childhood demonstrating how international comparisons can highlight many taken-for-granted notions which underpin practice. Most theories about childhood are based on the experiences of a minority of the world's children in wealthy countries such as those in Western Europe, the USA and Australia. This chapter draws attention to global inequalities and the ways in which children are dispro-portionately affected by the impact of globalisation. It emphasises the dangers of making universal assumptions about childhood based on expectations drawn from the developed world and shows how versions of childhood are dependent on economic circumstances.

The focus of Chapter 8 is the child's own perspective. Most knowledge and theory about children's lives is written or told from the perspective of adults so this chapter introduces the competing idea of 'child standpoint'. The concept of children as active social actors and social agents in their own right is examined and the difficulties and conflicts which arise in connection with ideas of competency are debated. The chapter also outlines ways in which practitioners can work respectfully with children to develop meaningful collaboration.

The final chapter of the book considers the twenty-first century context of childhood and the place of children within contemporary society. Although in the West children's lives have improved immeasurably in material terms over the past decades, there is at the same time an increasing anxiety about their well-being which takes many forms. Technology and consumerism are among the factors which have been blamed for the 'disappearance' of childhood and this chapter evaluates the extent to which such claims are valid. The way in which ideas of vulnerability position children as either victims or threats is examined to consider the implications of these discourses for children's lives in the twenty-first century and to challenge the moral panics which result in children being both overprotected and underestimated.

The pace of social change in the past 50 years has been phenomenal and there is every likelihood that society will continue to evolve as rapidly in the future. This has an impact on everyone's lives so it is essential to understand the processes and influences that affect the society we live in. But it is even more important to anyone working with children because they are in the front line of social change. The children of today will be the adults of tomorrow and the world they will inherit will be quite different to that in place now in the second decade of the twenty-first century. If we are to work effectively with and for children, then it is vital to have an understanding of the social processes and institutions that impact on childhood and the many different aspects which make up the context of children's lives.

1   The context of childhood

Through reading this chapter, you will:

- consider the difficulty of defining 'childhood' and how we determine who is considered to be a 'child';
- examine the conflict and ambiguities that are raised by these questions;
- understand why the social context is so critical to an understanding of childhood.

The chapter introduces Bronfenbrenner's model of development as a useful way of theorising the child within society.

Introduction

Until the final decades of the twentieth century the idea of childhood as a distinct and separate social category had been paid very little attention. Ideas *about* children have abounded throughout history (and will be explored further in Chapter 2) but children themselves were rarely considered important enough to warrant deliberate study. By the eighteenth century scientists, philosophers and educators had begun to systematically study children and build up knowledge about them. Since then ideas about how children grow, the developmental stages they go through and different theories of how language is acquired have emerged as subjects of study within such fields as psychology, education and health. Thus there is now a well-established body of knowledge known as child development which is studied by all those interested in working with children. However, until recently the existence of a stage in human lifespan which we call 'childhood' was simply taken for granted and the concept itself rarely examined or questioned.

What is childhood?

Every adult was once a child; it is the one defining characteristic that each of us has in common regardless of the myriad differences that make us unique individuals. This ought to make it a fairly simple matter to understand exactly what childhood is and what the term signifies. However, the more we try to pin down and identify exactly what we mean by childhood, the more slippery a concept it turns out to be. The difficulties this presents help to illustrate why childhood is a cultural and social invention and why it is so important to understand the *context of childhood*.

ACTIVITY 1

Take a moment or two to try and define the concept of 'child' yourself.

Complete the following sentences:

- *A child is …*

- *Childhood is …*

Write down your definitions on a piece of paper before continuing with this section.

The following are examples of some of the answers students have come up with when completing this exercise. Perhaps you thought of something similar?

- *A child is a small being who has not yet fully grown.*

- *A child is someone who is still learning.*

- *A child is a young person who is developing socially, emotionally, physically and cognitively.*

- *A child is someone in the vulnerable stage of life when they are still developing.*

- *A child is someone who needs to be nurtured and cared for until they are mature enough to look after themselves.*

It is noticeable that definitions such as these are primarily based on concepts of growth and development – they imply a being who is still incomplete and unfinished. This is a frequent theme that underpins the way in which children are understood and treated within contemporary society and will be explored in later chapters. Another idea apparent here is that of vulnerability and the need for care and nurturing – this is also something we can recognise as an underlying concern and is key to understanding adult responses to children. Although nobody would wish to argue against the care and nurturing of young children, the notion of them as vulnerable and incomplete which these views suggest are frequently used to justify the regulation and control of children.

None of these definitions in themselves can help to identify a child; indeed some could just as well describe any young creature from a kitten to a tadpole. Definitions which do recognise that there is something essentially human about the category 'child' are nonetheless dependent on prior understanding of the finished product, in other words the adult. This demonstrates how it is essential to have an appreciation of human culture and society to begin to recognise the categories we apply to society and, importantly, the expectations which arise from them.

Ideas of development also suggest that once children have grown then they are no longer regarded as children, and yet a moment's thought can easily bring to mind discrepancies which undermine this view. Young people are frequently fully grown and could be viewed as perfectly capable of looking after themselves at some stage during secondary school and yet our society still considers them immature and labels them children. (This view of children has not always been the case and will be explored further in Chapter 2.) Nowadays we also have different ideas about learning and think of it as a lifelong project, certainly not something that can be regarded as complete at a particular stage of life. Consider also the situation of children in less economically developed countries where often very young children are expected to take on responsibilities, such as caring for younger siblings or earning money to support the family. (Global perspectives of childhood are considered more fully in Chapter 7.) Street children in Brazil living on the street and fending for themselves at an age when a British child would not yet have started formal schooling similarly disturb our cosy and comfortable ideas of the child and challenge us to think more broadly. Now look again at how you defined a child earlier on – are you satisfied that your definition is convincing or can you see problems with it?

Childhood as a social construction

If it is hard to determine precisely what we mean when we use the term 'child', then even more difficulties occur with an attempt to define 'childhood'. Turning to a dictionary for an answer, you are likely to be confronted with something along the lines of *childhood: the state of being a child* (this is from Chambers but any dictionary will give similar suggestions). But although such a definition might at first seem unhelpful, it does actually hold the clue to the problem by demonstrating that no agreed definition of childhood can be established in itself, without reference to the social perceptions within which it is experienced. In other words, there is no meaningful definition of childhood that could hold true for all societies and cultures; it will always vary according to cultural norms and expectations. This is what is meant by the claim that childhood is a social construction, as Steve Wagg explains:

> *Childhood, like so many other vitally important aspects of social life – gender, health, youth and so on – [is] socially constructed. It [is], in other words, what members of particular societies, at particular times and in particular places, say it is.*
>
> (1992, p.10)

This means that childhood isn't 'natural' and should be carefully distinguished from biological immaturity (James and Prout, 1997). Therefore it is evident that there can be no single universal childhood which everybody experiences.

THEORY FOCUS

What is the difference between social construction and social constructivism?

The apparent similarity between these two terms means that they are often confused, but they actually refer to quite separate and distinct ideas.

Social construction is a sociological term that refers to the way in which social 'reality' arises through the meanings that people give to actions and situations. These meanings arise as a result of specific cultural expectations. Gender is a prime example of social construction – what are deemed to be 'natural' traits of males and females have varied throughout history and across the globe. As a result, we can see that what it means to be feminine is not a universally established way of behaving, but only what is expected

continued 7

of people in any given society at a specific time in history. Childhood can be seen to be socially constructed because the expectations and understanding of what it is to be a child are not universally fixed but are culturally specific and vary across time and location.

Social constructivism is a term from psychology and child development that refers to the way in which the child actively constructs knowledge for themselves within a social context through interaction with others. So Vygotsky is familiar to us as a social constructivist theorist; he drew attention to how children's learning is mediated through interaction with culture as well as the importance of more knowledgeable peers and adults to support a child's cognitive development.

In summary, social construction refers to the social institution of *childhood* whereas social constructivism is used in connection with the child as an individual.

Wagg's assertion is an important one. The emergence of the sociology of childhood during the 1980s and 1990s firmly established the social institution of childhood as separate from the natural biological unfolding of the infant – a perspective which had previously dominated understanding. Although there are clearly universal characteristics of childhood – for instance the development of emotional bonds and the fact that infants are dependent on others for physical care such as food and shelter – the ways in which these basic human needs are met are infinitely variable. As James and Prout put it:

> *The immaturity of children is a biological fact but the ways in which that immaturity is understood and made meaningful is a fact of culture.*
>
> (1997, p.7)

The idea that childhood is socially constructed should not be confused with the fact that children are the product of their social experiences. It is a statement about the category of people we understand as children rather than about individuals. So although your own experience of childhood is unique to you alone, most readers of this book will nonetheless share the experience of a late twentieth-century childhood in a Western post-industrial economy. That shared childhood is quite different to that experienced by, for instance, a Victorian child, a Japanese child or a refugee child.

Classifying the social category of childhood

Understanding the reasons why childhood is such an uncertain concept is one thing, but translating these ideas to everyday life is quite another. As there can be no universally agreed definition of childhood, then who is regarded as a child varies considerably within different contexts, and is dependent on social, cultural and economic factors (Frønes, 1994). Exploring the situations that arise as a result clearly demonstrates the socially constructed nature of childhood. Although we may all feel that we recognise a child when we see one, without some clear guidelines about who should be treated as a child and who notions of childhood apply to, it would be difficult for a modern, complex society to function. There are two main ways in which younger members of society are classified as children: biological (i.e. related to their physical development) and legal (in terms of laws and regulations which apply to specific ages).

Legal classification of childhood is the main way in which society attempts to regulate and order its youngest citizens. There are many events in life which are age dependent – for instance, the age at which people may marry, vote or go to certain categories of film. For this reason many people try to define children according to their chronological age.

ACTIVITY 2

Think about as many activities as you can that are governed by laws related to age, for instance learning to drive, getting married, going to the cinema ...

Is there any logical development between these different ages?

Do they represent things that you gradually develop the appropriate skills and judgement to undertake? Or do they seem to be just arbitrary decisions?

Find out what age limits apply to some of these actions in other countries. What do you notice about the differences? Do you agree with any of them? Do any of them surprise you?

There seems to be little logic about the varying definitions of legal age. This demonstrates how laws have developed over time and been made to fit the social norms and expectations of a given period. As a result there is often no systematic logic behind legal stipulations; they are all the result of human decision making. For instance, the age of consent (that is, the age at which people are deemed competent to agree to sex) is 16 in Britain and at that age young people may also marry, as long as their parents give consent. However, they cannot legally watch an 'X' rated film which depicts sexual acts until they reach 18. This demonstrates the way that different legal systems develop over time and are grounded in the social attitudes of the period.

A recent example of how the boundaries of childhood and adulthood have been legally challenged is the fact that the age of consent has only applied to all young people since 2001. Prior to this it was an offence for gay men to have sex until the age of 21. The difference in the age of consent arose as a result of the Victorian belief that young boys were more vulnerable to the unwanted attentions of older men than young girls were. This view stemmed from ideas about class and gender that seem completely outdated to contemporary minds but remained enshrined in British law throughout the twentieth century. The law was successfully challenged by a 16-year-old boy who took his case to the European Commission on Human Rights claiming the right to enjoy a sexual relationship without fear of criminal prosecution. His campaign eventually resulted in the age of consent being equalised for all (Stonewall, 2004) and is a good example of how the legal regulation of childhood can be contested and has changed over time.

Many people are surprised to find quite how many differences there are between different countries because we grow up taking our own social circumstances for granted. It is instructive to look at how these ideas are related rather than consider them in isolation.

For instance, in Spain the legal age of consent is 12 (provided neither partner is over 18 to protect minors from exploitation) whereas the age at which young people are considered criminally responsible is 15 (in most of the UK it is ten). In the USA young people are allowed to drive at 16 and are able to use firearms before they may legally drink alcohol, which in many states is not until the age of 21. These differing perspectives can tell us about the social values of different countries; for instance, it could be argued that the UK seems to trust young people to make their own decisions considerably less than some other cultures do (in relation to sexuality for instance) and that we take a much harsher view of children, punishing them more severely and at an earlier age, than many other countries.

So can the difficulties of legally prescribed age limits be overcome if we consider development and growth as a marker of status instead? Amusement parks and fairgrounds frequently use size to determine who may and may not use certain equipment. Some rides are forbidden until children reach a specified height while other areas may only be available for those *under* a certain height restriction. The fact that size and age are frequently correlated is evident in children's clothes where a T-shirt is labelled for 2–3 years; toys and books with age recommendations demonstrate how expectations of development are also linked to chronological age.

Childhood professionals are very aware of these developmental 'norms' which are used to measure a child's progress; familiarity with these and the ability to recognise when a child diverges from them is an important skill. Such measures range from the milestones used to check when infants sit up, crawl, walk and say their first word to tests such as the controversial end-of-key-stage tests which identify school children's progress against agreed criteria. Of course these measures do have a use and familiarity with them is important, but it is also essential to recognise that all norms and standards are culturally specific and however much we might measure and observe children this cannot reveal any fundamental 'truths' about childhood. Interpretation of the 'facts' is dependent on the explanations we give them – and that is informed by attitudes and beliefs that have been shaped by social experience.

ACTIVITY 3

Childhood obesity has been a subject of considerable concern both in the UK and the USA for some years and there has been a range of initiatives designed to tackle it. In May 2009 the Royal College of Paediatrics and Child Health (RCPCH) introduced revised baby weight charts. The RCPCH was commissioned to design new charts reflecting the average growth of breast-fed babies to replace previous growth charts calculated for babies predominantly fed with formula. The intention behind this was to encourage mothers to breastfeed their children – generally agreed to give babies a much healthier start in life. Babies who are breastfed gain weight more slowly and are less likely to become obese. To reflect this the revised charts reduced 'expected' weight gain during the first year downwards by a kilogram in line with the slower increase associated with breastfeeding. The intention was to remove women's anxiety that their breastfed babies are 'underweight' and to discourage the rapid weight gain that could be an early indicator of obesity.

Consider the implications of this measure and the effects for parents, for health visitors and paediatric nurses and for practitioners in nurseries and Early Years centres.

What does it demonstrate about our knowledge of children?

This example illustrates the way in which apparently objective, scientific facts about children's development are dependent on social context and cannot be understood without taking this into account. It demonstrates how advised 'average' and 'ideal' weights are simply numbers agreed by chosen experts working within a particular social context and shows that ideas about obesity are culturally dependent notions rather than objective truths. The recommended weight for a specific age could thus change overnight and so awareness of the wider context is essential because too strict a focus on normative expectations can be misleading. The problem with developmental classification of childhood is that it rests on the idea of an average child and such a being is unlikely to ever exist in reality. As Rose (1989) suggests:

> The 'normal' child is in fact a curious mix of statistical averages and historically specific value judgements. The most striking aspect of the 'normal' child is how abnormal he or she is, since there is no such person in reality and never has been. The advantage of defining normality is that it is a device that enables those in control or in charge to define, classify and treat those who do not seem to fit in.
>
> (cited in Penn, 2005, p.7)

Examining childhood in its context

Social attitudes do not stand still and as a result there are many contradictions and disagreements about the nature of children, what constitutes the state of childhood and how children should be treated and responded to. One of the aims of this book is to help you recognise these ideas and perspectives for yourself, to understand how they have come about and to be able to challenge them too, when appropriate or necessary.

Some persistent ideas about childhood have already been raised earlier in attempts to define the child. For instance, the view that children are particularly vulnerable and in need of protection underpins many of our attitudes as a society towards children. However, although this idea is widespread, there are also occasions when the media have caused people to feel fearful of children so that talk has turned to protecting society from children rather than the other way around. So individual children are likely to experience a range of conflicting social attitudes and expectations at different times and in different circumstances.

One of the ideas most frequently associated with children is the concept of innocence which will be explored more fully in Chapter 2. The rosy assumption of presumed innocence lies behind a perceived need to protect children and concerns about the 'loss' of such innocence lead to regulation and control. So protection can be a double-edged sword; while some view childhood as an idyllic garden where carefree children have the liberty to frolic and play, others have viewed childhood as being more like a prison, a social space within which children are confined and restricted and which they cannot escape until they grow up (Holt, 1975). These underlying assumptions affect the ways in which people respond to children and have serious consequences for what is considered to be a 'proper' childhood, but they are usually just taken for granted and rarely questioned. One of the most important aspects of studying childhood is to recognise the implications of these attitudes and beliefs and to develop your own value base and philosophy of childhood.

Whichever of these perspectives you are most inclined to, it is evident that adults are the gatekeepers who hold the keys to adulthood and full participation within society. The cultural recognition of maturity is called the age of majority and every society has its own rules and regulations about what this entails. In Britain, even though the age of majority was lowered from 21 to 18 more than thirty years ago, cultural remnants are still apparent in the importance attached to twenty-first birthday celebrations. Although, as we have seen, there are certain rights which may be conferred prior to this, until the age of majority children are considered by the state to be minors and their life is determined by the adults around them. In recent years there has been growing awareness of the child's own perspective and the 1989 Children Act laid down in law that children's views must be taken into account in decisions affecting their lives. How successful this aspiration is in reality is examined in Chapter 8.

Bronfenbrenner's sociocultural model of development

Urie Bronfenbrenner's concept of the 'ecological niche' is a very useful way to think about and analyse the context of childhood. Bronfenbrenner's book *The Two Worlds of Childhood* (1972) compared and contrasted the experience of childhood in the United States and what was then called the Union of Soviet Socialist Republics (USSR; now split up into Russia and neighbouring countries such as Ukraine). He later built on these ideas to develop more generalised principles which he termed an ecological model of childhood (1979). Ecology is the name given to the study of people or institutions in relation to their environment so Bronfenbrenner's model considers the way in which different environmental systems, including social, cultural, economic and political factors, impact on human development. This has been a very influential idea in shaping how people theorise and explain the social context of children's lives.

Bronfenbrenner portrays human development as influenced by a range of interrelated systems which impact on the child. He likened this to a set of Russian dolls where each sits within another although that metaphor can underplay the role of the child, hidden away within the outlying systems that make up their everyday experiences. Bronfenbrenner would reject the implication of a one-way socialisation process in which the child is a passive recipient of social information and emphasised the way in which the influence of the various systems is two directional (Figure 1). Modern recognition of the child as a social actor in their own right supports this active influence and is explored in Chapter 8.

The *microsystem* is the context in which the child's earliest experiences take place. For the majority of children, the immediate family, i.e. parents or carers and siblings, are the first relationships they form and remain central to their lives. However, a very large proportion of children experience more than one microsystem and may spend a considerable part of their daily lives within a setting such as a nursery or childminder's house as well as their own home.

Chronosystem
The long-term context of
historical changes which impact
on social factors at all levels

Macrosystem
The broader context of social structures,
political ideology, economic forces and
wider value and belief systems

Exosystem
The localised context or community
within which micro- and meso-
systems exist

Mesosystems
The interaction and communication
between the child's various microsystems

Microsystem – family
the child's immediate context where all their
first experiences are mediated. The microsystem
is impacted on by all the surrounding levels,
e.g. local and national

Microsystem – the setting
Nowadays most children spend a large proportion
of their time within different settings which form a
major site of socialisation

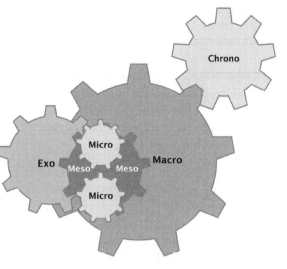

Figure A dynamic model of the ecological niche
(adapted from Bronfenbrenner, 1979 and 1986)

Growing up in an extended family will also affect the nature of the child's microsystem(s). Bronfenbrenner uses the term *mesosystem* to refer to the interaction and relationships between the various microsystems in the child's life. He emphasises the importance of the mesosystem and of good partnership between the various parties to support the child's transitions between these.

The *exosystem* is the wider environment within which micro- and meso-systems exist. This is the local context or community which will impact on the child's experience through such things as opportunities for parental employment, local authority organisation and regional socio-economic factors. It is easy to recognise that a child growing up in the countryside has very different experiences to an urban child but there are many other less visible differences such as the extent to which children are integrated into their local community. Ethnic or religious background may also affect this, for instance if a child attends their local church or mosque.

Beyond the exosystem lies the *macrosystem* which is the arena of wider political and ideological beliefs, social values and customs. This influence is sometimes obvious, such as when new legislation affecting the child is introduced; this is the result of government strategies and priorities and is swayed by political ideology. Other times its influence is hidden and more ambiguous. For instance, underlying social attitudes, such as ideas about appropriate ways for families to behave, views of working mothers and the effect of the media, all affect the environment in which the child is socialised. Changes within the macrosystem, although far removed from individual children's lives, have many implications for how education and childcare is organised and how resources and budgets are allocated. These changes may take place at a national or international level; for instance in 1989 the UK signed up to the United Nations Convention on the Rights of the Child (UNCRC) which has not only affected policies and legislation regarding children but also impacted on the way professionals view the child.

The final aspect of this model is the *chronosystem* (Bronfenbrenner, 1986) which relates to the sociohistorical conditions of childhood; in other words the way in which all of these social factors are mediated by their historical period. For instance, it has already been noted that a large proportion of children growing up today spend a considerable period of each day in daycare. This is unlikely to have been the experience of most of today's adults and is the result of wider economic factors affecting employment patterns as well as changing perceptions of the role of women. Another example of the chronosystem is the impact of technology which has completely altered the landscape of childhood in recent years.

ACTIVITY 4

Take a large sheet of paper and draw a set of concentric circles to represent Bronfenbrenner's ecological model of development.

Think of a child who you know well and note on your diagram how the various ecological systems affect the child's experience of childhood.

When you have completed this, consider how these might vary for (a) a child in care, (b) a child of divorced parents, (c) an immigrant child, and (d) a nine-month-old baby whose parents have full-time jobs and who attends day care.

What are the main differences that you have noted?

What are the consequences of this variation in terms of childhood?

It is important to recognise that the influence of this ecological model is two directional and works not just from the macro down to the micro but also applies the other way. For instance, although national policy is made centrally and passed down to local and individual levels, it can be influenced and challenged. An illustration of this is the way in which childhood practitioners and academics were consulted about the Early Years Foundation Stage (DfES, 2007) and so had an opportunity to feed into and shape government policy.

Bronfenbrenner's model helps us to understand and recognise the different contexts which impact on childhood. This can help support understanding of what childhood is, what it means and the ways we behave towards children as a result. This ecological model of childhood has been used as a framework for much of this book so that individual chapters relate to particular aspects of the ecological system. Chapters 3 and 4 focus on the microsystems of the family and the setting and also raise issues about the mesosystem surrounding them. Chapter 5, 'The community context', examines the exosystem and ways in which local factors impact on how childhood is experienced. Chapters 6 and 7 are both focused on the wider macrosystem and seek to explain the significance of this for the phenomenon of childhood. Chapters 8 and 9 interconnect the different levels of Bronfenbrenner's model so that it can be recognised how the context of childhood is fluid and changeable. The chronosystem is evident in Chapter 2, which examines the way that ideas about childhood have changed over time, as well as in the historical time line (page 121) which identifies key changes which have affected the context of childhood.

Conclusion

Neil Postman, whose ideas will be explored in the following chapter, suggested that adulthood should be viewed as a symbolic rather than a biological achievement (1994). This demonstrates of course that adulthood is just as much a social construction as childhood – in fact one cannot be present without the other because they exist only in relation to each other. These age divisions are not 'natural' but are socially defined and simply denote customary ways of viewing categories of people. The way such categories arise and come to be accepted as normal stages of life may be easier to understand through the example of how teenagers were 'invented' in the decade following the Second World War. Before this period adolescents were generally viewed as young people at the beginning of their adult lives. Most would have left school by age 15 and their earnings made a welcome contribution to the family income; for instance, wartime ration books noted a category of 'men and women under 18 years'. However, the growing prosperity of the post-war years meant young people could keep more of their wages to spend on themselves. As they were increasingly able to buy records and clothes and go to the cinema, manufacturers began to recognise the value of the new teenage market and to create new products to cater for it. Nowadays the teenager is a well-established social category and other subgroups are starting to be recognised such as the pre-teens dubbed 'tweens'.

The last two centuries have seen dramatic changes in conceptions of childhood in children's culture, child-rearing practices, family life and adult–child relationships. To really understand the place of childhood within contemporary society it is important to be able to look through other eyes and recognise how different mindsets alter the perception of 'reality' and what is considered normal. This can help us keep open the question of what childhood actually denotes and recognise the fluidity and ambiguity of the concept.

SUMMARY

This chapter has considered the socially constructed nature of childhood and the ways in which it might be regarded as a cultural invention. Although all human infants have certain needs and characteristics in common, the way in which adults respond to these and the meanings they attach to them is variable and dependent on cultural norms. Thus there can be no universal definition and the experience of childhood needs to be recognised as a social phenomenon.

---

continued

SUMMARY *continued*

The variable nature of the social category called childhood is problematic when society tries to apply rules and regulations to minors. Laws and statutory frameworks use age as a marker, intended as an objective measure that can be applied fairly to everyone. However, it is evident that because regulations develop over time and are affected by current social values and beliefs, there is little logical coherence or relationship between different conventions. Expectations about biological development are equally difficult and open to challenge.

The way in which society treats its youngest citizens is dependent on assumptions and beliefs about the nature of childhood which are often unexamined and contradictory. This has real consequences for children's experience of life because it is adults' views of 'the child' which underpin ideas of what should be provided for children and what constitutes a proper childhood. Children's lives are regulated by the adults around them, whether these are their family, the practitioners in settings they attend, or politicians drafting legislation that affects their lives. Bronfenbrenner's ecological model of development helps to illustrate the way in which all these different social systems interact and impact on the child's experience.

FURTHER READING

James, A and James, A (2004) *Constructing childhood: theory, policy and social practice.* Basingstoke: Palgrave Macmillan.

An important text in the new social studies of childhood, this book examines the ways in which childhood is constructed in contemporary society and the implications this has for the lives of real children. Four case studies (covering education, health, crime and the family) demonstrate how ideas about childhood frame law and policy.

James, A and James, A (2008) *Key concepts in childhood studies.* London: Sage

A really useful little book that defines and explains key concepts such as social construction, childhood and many other terms you will come across in this book.

Waller, T (2009) Modern childhood: contemporary theories and children's lives, in Waller, T (ed) *An introduction to early childhood: a multidisciplinary approach.* 2nd edition. London: Sage

This chapter is a very accessible discussion of the multiple perspectives of childhood and differing contexts of children's lives. Waller emphasises the importance of recognising the ways in which children play an active role in constructing their childhood and identifies how this perspective has affected childhood studies.

Wyness, M (2006) *Childhood and society: an introduction to the sociology of childhood.* Basingstoke: Palgrave.

A clear and detailed overview of the range of approaches sociologists have employed in examining the phenomenon of childhood. Wyness covers all the key debates including the social meaning of childhood, the privatisation of childhood, regulating childhood and children as social agents.

2   The historical context

Through reading this chapter, you will:

- consider the extent to which childhood may be understood as a modern phenomenon;
- examine the experience of childhood in its historical perspective;
- recognise the continuing influence of various discourses in shaping ideas about the nature of childhood;
- examine the historical process by which children moved out of the workforce and into schooling;
- understand the development of modern concepts of childhood.

Introduction

Chapter 1 introduced the idea of childhood as a social construction, in other words as something which is shaped by the ideas and expectations of society. This chapter examines the development of ideas about childhood since the Middle Ages and the ways in which attitudes towards children and the experience of childhood have changed over that period.

The invention of childhood

The socially constructed nature of childhood suggests that it can only exist within societies which recognise such a concept. This raises the intriguing idea that childhood may not always be present in the social order. So have children always existed? This is not quite such a nonsensical question as it first appears and there are a number of reasons to argue that childhood is in fact a modern invention.

Two important writers who have argued this case are Philippe Ariès (1986) and Neil Postman (1994) who both suggest that childhood is a modern phenomenon that has only come into being in relatively recent times.

At first such a notion may seem nonsense because clearly people have always reproduced and given birth to children, otherwise the human race would have died out long ago. But human reproduction is not the same thing as a separate social category of 'childhood'. Ariès and Postman argue that in the past the young were not understood as children in the way we now understand the term. They were not treated any differently nor recognised as being in need of particular concern because of their young age.

Ariès suggests that:

> *in medieval society the idea of childhood did not exist; this is not to suggest that children were neglected, forsaken or despised. The idea of childhood is not to be confused with affection for children: it corresponds to an awareness of the particular nature of childhood, that particular nature which distinguishes the child from the adult, even the young adult. In medieval society this awareness was lacking.*
>
> (1986, p.125)

Here Ariès is claiming that although children may well have been treated with affection, they were simply perceived as undeveloped adults. Children lived and worked alongside adults, wearing the same clothes and undertaking the same activities. There was no concept of 'development' and children learned about life by participating in it. At a time when most adults were illiterate, entertainment and leisure pursuits would have been very similar for all ages and he suggests that as soon as the child *could live without the constant solicitude of his mother, his nurse or his cradle rocker then he belonged to adult society* (1986, p.125). Ariès draws his evidence from historical documents and paintings but his conclusions have been challenged by a number of critics. For instance, Tucker (1977) points out that we have no way of knowing how children were viewed by their mothers and nurses as the majority of surviving historical evidence was produced by men.

Neil Postman concurred with Ariès' thesis about the modern invention of childhood claiming that *there is ample evidence that children have existed for less than four hundred years* (1994, p.xi). However, he maintains that the invention of childhood was primarily due to the development of technology, namely the printing press around 1450. Before printing, Postman argues, communication was mainly through word of mouth so that once children had command of language there was little difference in the knowledge of adults and children. As a result, children were not seen as a separate social category who needed to prepare for adult life. However, as the introduction of printing spread rapidly throughout Europe and books which had previously been laboriously hand copied by monks could now be reproduced with relative ease, a world of abstract knowledge and new ideas was opened up. Postman argued that, as a result, childhood began to be viewed as a separate time set apart for learning.

ACTIVITY 1

Postman's theory is an interesting one but is open to challenge.

Postman suggests that the 'invention' of childhood resulted from the development of the printing press, with the result that children needed a time of education in order to learn to read and therefore be able to access the knowledge of their society.

Do you think that literacy is a sufficient explanation to account for a new social category, such as childhood, arising? If not, what other factors would need to be taken into account?

It is only in recent years that adult literacy has become more or less universal in this country. Would an adult who could not read or write still be considered as an adult?

*ACTIVITY **1*** *continued*

In what ways is Postman's account a Eurocentric explanation? For instance, in many areas of the world there remain high levels of adult illiteracy – to what extent might this affect social relationships between adults and children?

Postman developed his thesis further to argue that another change in communication technology, namely television, is now bringing about the 'disappearance' of childhood – this argument is considered in Chapter 9.

Pre-industrial childhood in the early modern period

Ariès' main concern was to trace the development of the modern family and the way in which the shared communal life of the medieval period had, by the seventeenth century, been gradually replaced by 'the wall of private life'. This change in the way living arrangements were ordered was also bolstered by religious ideas about morality and the importance of impressing habits of obedience and discipline on children. Infants began to be seen as 'fragile creatures of God who needed to be both safeguarded and reformed' (Ariès, 1986, p.396).

Religion has always had a great influence on how children are viewed. At a time when so many children did not survive infancy, the importance of baptism to ensure that a child's soul would go straight to heaven cannot be overemphasised. Parents were seen to have an obligation to save children from their natural wickedness and an increasing emphasis on children's religious duty arose, especially under the influence of the Puritans. Children were expected to learn prayers and the catechism by heart and the prime reason for learning to read was so as to be able to read the Bible. Much of this attitude towards children was based on ideas of original sin and the implications of this as a discourse are discussed in the next section of this chapter.

Without modern standards of sanitation and medicine a quarter of children were likely to die before their first birthday (Cunningham, 2006). Ariès suggests that adults made little emotional investment in their children because of the very real possibility of their loss at any time. It is a widespread assumption, therefore, that adults did not care for their offspring. However, Linda Pollock (1983) has challenged this view and shows that because parents did not view their children in the same way as contemporary parents does not mean that they did not love them. Certainly it is true that children were not idealised and sentimentalised as became commonplace in Victorian times, but there is ample evidence of warm and loving family relationships from diaries and historical accounts.

Throughout the seventeenth century childhood began to be more recognised with special clothing, books and playthings produced for children, as well as a number of books written to advise and guide parents. The book which had the greatest impact was written in 1692 by John Locke, a prominent philosopher of the period. Locke's ideas are most familiar within childhood studies from his *Essay Concerning Human Understanding* which put forward the view that the human mind is a *'tabula rasa'*, or a blank sheet, and that all ideas are derived from experience. In this he rejected the idea, common at the time, that children were innately bad and needed careful correction. When a friend sought Locke's advice regarding the upbringing of his son, he wrote him a series of letters, later to be published in book form. Entitled *Some Thoughts Concerning Education* this became hugely influential, running through nearly thirty editions over the next century and being translated into many European languages.

Locke stressed the importance of moulding the young from an early age through strict discipline, although he advocated developing self-control and a sound moral sense by reason rather than physical punishment. He also suggested that children could learn much through play, such as rolling a ball with letters pasted on it to become familiar with the alphabet. The huge success of Locke's book demonstrates that by this time there was clear recognition, at least among some classes, of children as distinctly different to adults and needful of care and consideration.

Throughout the sixteenth and seventeenth centuries a growing middle class had arisen whose increasing affluence enabled them to keep their children sheltered from the economy until a later age. These children were able to experience a protected period of life more akin to what we would now regard as childhood. Nonetheless, for the vast majority, it was taken for granted that children should work and contribute to the family upkeep. As well as an economic necessity, work was also considered an appropriate way to keep the young usefully occupied and out of mischief. The nature of the work would vary according to the parents' occupation and regional industry. For instance, young girls in Nottingham would be engaged, alongside their mothers, in making lace whereas children in areas of wool production would learn to spin, card and weave. In the countryside children were employed in stone clearing and crow scaring and would be expected to help with harvesting and agricultural tasks such as caring for animals. This expectation for rural children continued much longer than other forms of child labour, demonstrating that childhood is always mediated by geography as well as factors such as class, gender and ethnicity.

The Enlightenment

The Enlightenment, or the Age of Reason, was an intellectual movement which spread across Europe during the eighteenth century. Inspired in part by the ideas of scholars such as Locke, Enlightenment thinkers rejected the irrational superstitions which, in their view, had governed life in the Middle Ages. The development of scientific enquiry and the idea of Man as rational and fundamentally good (women were rarely considered worthy of note at the time) opened up the possibility of human progress and a more just society. Many concepts regarded as central to modern democratic societies, such as equality and liberty, can be traced to the Enlightenment and with them a growing sense of the child as innocent rather than simply ignorant.

One of most influential thinkers of this period was Jean-Jacques Rousseau. Although Swiss by birth, Rousseau spent much of his adult life in Paris where his writings about liberty were current at the time of the French Revolution. However, it was his book *Emile*, published in 1762, which is particularly significant in the history of childhood. One of Rousseau's central themes is that Man is born good but corrupted by society and *Emile*, a fictional account of a boy educated by his tutor, described his ideas of how a different type of society could be cultivated through education. Emile is brought up in the country, far from the contaminating influences of society, in such a way as to encourage his instinctive impulses and curiosity and to avoid interfering with his natural state. Rousseau suggested that:

> *Nature wants children to be children before they are men. If we deliberately depart from this order we shall get premature fruits which are neither ripe nor well flavoured and which soon decay ... Childhood has ways of seeing, thinking and feeling peculiar to itself; nothing can be more foolish than to seek to substitute our ways for them.*
>
> (1974, p.55)

Rousseau advocated that the teacher should always follow the child's interests because this was how nature ensured children learned what they needed to know. He complained that people were too often concerned to *devote themselves to what a man ought to know without asking what a child is capable of learning* (1974, p.1). Like Locke, Rousseau's underlying assumption was that education should be a matter primarily for boys although he does include a young girl, Sylvie, as an appropriate companion for the adult Emile. However, Sylvie's far more limited role simply prepares her to become a suitable wife, for Rousseau believed that *[t]he man should be strong and active; the woman should be weak and passive* (1974, p.322). This shows how ideas about childhood have developed unevenly and subject to other discourses such as gender.

ACTIVITY 2

Some of Locke and Rousseau's ideas appear outlandish today but many of their underlying principles are still prevalent. They had some ideas in common – for instance, both rejected the idea that children were innately wicked and proposed what would now seem harsh measures intended to physically toughen children. However, overall they were very different in their fundamental philosophy. Locke saw children as very impressionable and therefore needing to be set in good habits for the future. He held that learning could be made more interesting through games, whereas Rousseau believed children should not be 'spoiled' by exposing them to planned learning. He thought children should be left to develop according to their natural inclinations and that the teacher must observe them closely to identify what these might be.

What elements of Locke and Rousseau's thinking can you detect in contemporary ideas about children and childhood?

Emile was a hugely influential book becoming what would now be regarded as a 'bestseller' to the extent that, unable to keep up with demand, booksellers rented out copies by the hour. Although Rousseau had abandoned his own five children to an orphanage, his account of a 'natural' and unspoiled childhood had enormous emotional appeal and many people tried to bring up their children according to his principles.

Discourses of childhood

We have established that childhood is not a 'natural' state but shaped by how it is understood and represented within a society. Therefore the things we think we 'know' about children are not, as they seem to be, self-evident truths and facts about children but are always the products of human meaning-making. These meanings and representations come about through *discourse*, an accepted view or explanatory framework built up of ideas, concepts and beliefs. Discourses become established ways of understanding society and are embedded as 'knowledge'. Foucault (1977) argues that, therefore, discourses are not simply neutral ways of describing the world but carry immense social power in determining which versions of reality are accepted.

There are two main discourses which shape the understanding of childhood within Western societies. These are the *discourse of the innocent child* and the *discourse of the sinful child*. The discourse of the sinful child derives from the idea of original sin which has its roots in Christian doctrine. Original sin is the belief that all people inherit a state of sin through Adam and Eve's rebellion against God in the Garden of Eden. Such a view suggests children are born sinful and that their natural tendencies should be controlled and corrected so that they might grow into civilised adults. As John Bunyan wrote in *Pilgrim's Progress* in 1684:

> Their sinful Nature prompts them to rebel
> And to delight in Paths that lead to Hell.

Therefore good parents should aim to civilise children away from inherent evil beginning with baptism and continuing through strict discipline so that they learn to submit their will and desires to moral authority. The old adage 'Spare the rod and spoil the child' from a poem of Samuel Butler in 1664 can be seen as part of this discourse.

In contrast, the discourse of innocence suggests that children are inherently innocent and naturally good. This discourse frequently associates children with nature and representations of childhood innocence are common features of art and literature from this period. Poets such as Wordsworth and Blake represented children as pure beings untainted by worldly cares or concerns. Seen from this perspective, childhood is a special state which needs to be nurtured and protected and as such has strong symbolic significance for adults. Diana Gittins suggests that:

> We see in [children] qualities of innocence, purity, trust, beauty and joy, which we
> see in virtually no other phenomena – qualities which we feel, by becoming an
> adult, we have lost.

> (1998, p.1)

The discourse of innocence is of course a cultural view of the nature of childhood itself rather than a judgement about individual children's capabilities and potential. However, James and James (2008) warn of the slippage between these related concepts and suggest that the association between childhood and innocence can have many negative consequences for the actual lived experiences of real children.

It is customary to consider the discourse of the sinful child as prevalent in the time of the Puritans and later displaced by the discourse of innocence arising from the Enlightenment. However, Cunningham (2006) argues that both existed in various forms in early Christian thought for many centuries. It is also interesting to note that Western Romantic and Puritan discourses of childhood are echoed in traditional Chinese philosophy where Confucianism emphasises control and discipline in contrast to the Wang-ming approach of awakening the child through self-reflection (Wells, 2009).

Although Prout (2005) suggests that in order for childhood studies to progress, the time has come to move beyond simplistic dualisms which suggest something is wholly one thing or the other, nonetheless it is important to be alert to the power of these discourses which still influence how we perceive and deal with children as a society. Expectations and attitudes towards children in public policy and the media can be seen to be underpinned directly by both discourses.

While the influence of Enlightenment thought on the understanding of childhood is still discernible today, Rousseau's ideas had a direct impact on what is generally termed the Early Years tradition. The pioneer Pestalozzi, realising that a tutor who could devote himself entirely to one child was unrealistic, started his own school inspired by Rousseau's principles. This school became famous, attracting visitors from all over Europe including a young Austrian, Friedrich Froebel, whose kindergarten movement later became so influential. Thus a direct line can be traced from Rousseau to many of the principles under-pinning contemporary Early Years practice (Bruce, 2005).

The effects of industrialisation

One of the greatest impacts on the experience of childhood was undoubtedly the effect of industrialisation. Whereas previously children had largely worked alongside their parents within the family unit, the Industrial Revolution centralised production within factories and mills. Children's labour was particularly valuable in textile industries where their small size and nimble fingers enabled them to undertake tasks such as tying in threads which adults could not manage with such dexterity. They were also of course cheap to employ. In fact the cheapness of child labour contributed to Britain's industrial success throughout the eighteenth and nineteenth centuries and was used as an argument against control. Opponents of legislation claimed that child labour was essential to ensure the country could remain competitive in an international market.

A notable effect of industrialisation was a dramatic change in a way of life which had existed for centuries. Throughout the nineteenth century huge numbers of people were drawn from the countryside to the newly expanding towns and cities and the everyday life of the majority of the population became increasingly urban and industrial rather than rural and agricultural. An important aspect of this change was that traditional extended families, where several generations lived together collaborating economically to support each other, became replaced by smaller 'nuclear' family units. This demographic change was also reinforced by the example of the queen whose family life came to embody Victorian ideology as the standard of stability and respectability. By the end of the nineteenth century this domestic ideal of the family as a private haven centred around happily innocent children had taken a strong hold of the public imagination. At a time of substantial technological change and social upheaval this sentimentalised image of childhood was imbued with a nostalgic longing for a time of greater innocence and a simpler way of life. Thus it held a great symbolic significance for adults which remains to this day.

ACTIVITY 3

Look through the illustrations in books in the art history section of your library to find representations of children.

What clues can you find in the pictures about children's lives in the past?

Consider the dates when pictures were painted and see how you can connect this to what you know of childhood in that period.

If you live near a city with a large art gallery, pay a visit to look at the paintings on display. You are likely to find this most valuable if you go with a couple of others so that you can discuss your ideas together.

Childhood was a recurring theme in Victorian culture and authors such as Dickens and Charles Kingsley, whose *Water Babies* brought the plight of child chimney sweeps to public attention, helped raise awareness of the exploitation and harsh conditions which affected so many children. The issue of child labour began to be a matter of public concern and over the nineteenth century a number of government Acts introduced to regulate children's working conditions brought about gradual improvements. For instance, the Factory Act of 1833 made it illegal for children under nine to work in textile factories and limited the working hours of those aged between nine and 13. An earlier Factory Act in 1819 applying to child workers in cotton mills had had limited effect and so the new Act brought in factory inspectors to enforce the legislation. However, economic necessity meant that many parents lied about their children's age, an easy enough subterfuge before the legal requirement to register births (not introduced until 1837 in England and Wales, 1855 in Scotland and 1864 in Ireland). The 1833 Factory Act also stipulated a requirement that children over the age of nine working in factories and mills should have some form of part-time education. Legislation was gradually extended to cover working children in other industries, such as mining where the Mines Act of 1842 prohibited children under ten from working underground, raised to the age of 12 in 1860. This steady tightening of the labour laws gradually pushed children out of the world of work into more marginal employment opportunities such as errand boys and other informal jobs.

The problem of poor children

Another aspect of increased urbanisation was that it made poverty more visible. Children have always been among the poorest sections of the population and it is still the case that families with children suffer disproportionately from poverty (see Chapter 5). Historically children formed a much greater proportion of the population, for instance in the sixteenth century nearly a third of the population were under 15 (Cunningham, 1995) and this caused concern for their welfare as well as a fear of children wandering the countryside or begging in the streets. The Poor Relief Act of 1597 had made pauper children the responsibility of the parish and the subsequent Poor Law of 1601 remained the prime means of welfare for the next 200 years. In London the first distinct institution for orphans and abandoned children, Christ's Hospital, was founded in 1552. Similar initiatives followed later in other major towns with the idea that children should be set to work to earn their keep.

By the eighteenth century social reformers began to be concerned about improving conditions for poor children. Thomas Coram's Foundling Hospital, opened in 1744, is one of the most famous examples of such philanthropy and attracted the support of many rich and famous people as 'childsaving' became a popular concern among the fashionable classes. Children received rudimentary education and were placed as apprentices to learn a trade. However, poverty was such a widespread problem that charity alone could not solve the issue. One of the responses to the predicament was to send children out to the newly established colonies in Canada and Australia, a practice which continued until the 1960s.

By the nineteenth century the growing interest in children and childhood began to make the massive gulf between the lives of rich and poor more evident and this is the period during which many of the well-known organisations for children were founded. For instance, Dr Barnardo established his first home for destitute children in 1870 and the National Society for the Prevention of Cruelty to Children (NSPCC) was founded in 1884.

The introduction of full-time schooling

The idea of schooling as the full-time and compulsory occupation of children is a concept that has existed for less than 150 years. In 1868, Joseph Chamberlain, mayor of Birmingham, set up a National Education League to campaign for free, secular (i.e. not connected to the Church) and compulsory schooling. Although there were still those who were opposed to education of the lower orders, by this time many people were beginning to believe that children under ten should be occupied in some form of schooling. Many shared the humanitarian ideals of the education league but others were more concerned with schooling as a means of control and discipline. Despite the actions of many social reformers, as child labour became increasingly restricted there were more and more children visible on the streets. Children's idleness and the threat that the children of the poor represented to the 'respectable' classes continued to be a matter of public concern and school began to be seen as the most appropriate solution.

The Forster Education Act of 1870 was a landmark piece of legislation in regard to educational provision because for the first time it made elementary education available to all children up to the age of ten. It is not of course the case that children had received no education until this time but what they experienced depended very much on their background. While wealthy children had private tutors and governesses, schooling could be minimal or non-existent for the poor and always regarded as something to be fitted around the more important demands of work. The 1833 Factory Act had ensured that children working in textile industries received some form of education and this applied also to those children cared for under the Poor Laws but there was no provision for others. Some children attended privately run 'dame schools', Sunday school or charitable Christian schools but this was dependent on where they lived and standards could be very low. Cunningham (2003) traces the gradual rise of literacy throughout the nineteenth century from marriage registers where two-thirds of men and half of their brides were able to sign their names in the 1830s. This gradually rose to 95 per cent by the end of the century when education had become compulsory.

The Forster Act set up School Boards in each area to fill the gaps where there were insufficient voluntary schools run by the Church. Schooling was accepted more willingly by some than others. Many of the poor could see no benefit in education which could do little to improve their children's life chances. They were understandably reluctant to send children who might be earning money to school; a situation aggravated by the need to pay school fees. Although this might only be a penny or tuppence per child it represented an additional burden to poor families. School Boards were able to make attendance compulsory if they chose and over the next decade this gradually spread until it became universal by 1880. School attendance officers were appointed in every district to enforce attendance and parents were taken to court and fined for not ensuring their children went to school. However, it was not until the Education Act of 1891 that schooling became free for all children.

Parents were particularly likely to keep their children off school when they were needed to help out at home and recognition of the importance of this is evident in the establishment of the school year with long summer holidays to coincide with the harvest. By the end of the nineteenth century, however, greater economic well-being had strengthened the acceptance of full-time education for children and the school leaving age was gradually raised to 11 in 1893 and then 12 in 1899. However, the contrast with Scotland, where elementary schools financed through the rates had existed in each parish since the late seventeenth century, shows that the growth of schooling was not simply a matter of financial circumstances. Scotland had a long tradition of valuing education and the Scottish equivalent of the Forster Act brought in compulsory schooling in 1872 for children up to the age of 13.

The Industrial Revolution often entailed misery and terrible conditions for huge numbers of children, but the social consequences completely changed the landscape of childhood. Indeed, Cunningham suggests that the changes of the past 200 years *amount to something like a revolution* (2003, p.82). By the end of the Victorian era, compulsory schooling which brought about increased state intervention in families' lives had begun to impose a standardised childhood and a certain concept of respectability on poor families. Working-class children's independence and self-reliance was increasingly controlled and limited and the middle-class experience of childhood gradually extended to become the accepted norm for all. Hendrick suggests that:

> … *by compulsorily keeping children within the classroom, schooling lengthened the years of 'childhood', while simultaneously reinforcing notions of the characteristics that were said to constitute* proper *childhood, namely ignorance, innocence and dependence. In this way, the* concept *of childhood (especially for working class children) was altered.*
>
> (original emphases,1997b, p.64)

The twentieth century

By the beginning of the twentieth century a modern concept of the child, characterised by a state of dependency, was emerging which would be recognisable to us now.
Throughout the rest of the century the ideal of childhood established during the Victorian
period was accompanied by growing scientific knowledge to enable childhood to
become increasingly regulated. To some extent this was a positive movement as children,
alongside the population as a whole, became progressively healthier and more attention
was paid to their needs. More legislation was passed in respect of children during the
twentieth century than in all previous centuries combined. On the other hand it has also
served to bring children increasingly under the regulation of the state and to establish
a proscribed view of what childhood should be. This continues to apply in particular to
children from lower socio-economic groups.

Improved medicine and public health measures had by this time ensured that children's
physical health was greatly improved and infant mortality had dropped dramatically.
Attention now turned to children's minds. By the end of the nineteenth century a Child
Study movement had begun to develop, intent on studying children scientifically and
Hendrick (1997a) suggests that schools were 'crucial' to this project by making children
available to professionals such as psychologists, doctors and educationalists. Throughout
the twentieth century child clinics grew rapidly and through them the idea of 'norms'
identifying what might be expected of children at particular ages and stages (Foley, 2001).
'Experts' were available to advise on newly discovered topics such as thumb sucking and
temper tantrums and to 'adjust' children to conform to what became regarded as normal
behaviour (Hendrick, 1997a). Children's role as investment for the nation brought them
increasingly under the gaze of medicine, education, law and welfare. The intervention of
the state is particularly evident in the mass evacuation of children from the cities during
the Second World War. This action brought to light the state of poverty and deprivation
affecting many children's lives and was one of the factors contributing to the post-war
development of the welfare state (see Chapter 6).

The expectation of children's contribution to the family economy, once taken for granted,
gradually disappeared during the twentieth century. In its place the normative experience
for children became schooling which by now was not only compulsory but also considerably extended in length. The school leaving age continued to rise (15 in 1944 later
increased to 16 in 1973) and with it the years of childhood.

ACTIVITY 4

Educational provision has now been extended into the Early Years.

There is also a current proposal to raise the school leaving age to18 by 2013.

Do these initiatives change the nature of childhood in any way?

To what extent are aspects of schooling as a means of social control still visible?

*Qvortrup (1994) has argued that school children are not in fact removed from the labour
market but are still engaged in economically productive work. He suggests that during
their years in school children are occupied in producing their future working selves.*

In what ways can children's education be regarded as 'labour'?

As children ceased to be considered as significant contributors to the family purse, attitudes towards them changed and they began to be viewed as the focus for emotional expression instead. Tracing the development of the *economically useless but emotionally priceless* child in the twentieth century Zelizer (1994) suggests that:

> *True parental love could only exist if the child was defined exclusively as an object of sentiment and not as an agent of production.*

> (1994, p.72)

This twentieth-century model of childhood would have been unrecognisable to most people, children included, in the past.

THEORY FOCUS

Generation

One of the consequences of the modern construction of childhood is that it strengthens social divisions based on age. As children have become increasingly separated from society in schools, nurseries and other forms of childcare, there is a clearer demarcation between adults and children. Social relationships have progressively come to be determined by intra-generational links (i.e. within a generation) rather than being intergenerational or cross generational. The relationships between children and adults have changed significantly since the Second World War and Foley (2008a) suggests that one of the paradoxes of childhood is that the generation gap might be argued to be both expanding and narrowing.

Generation is a term often used loosely to denote an age group, such as 'the younger generation', but James and James (2008) point out the importance of generation as the shared location of a group of people in a historical time. Different generations' contrasting conditions of life are evident from the account of childhood examined in this chapter, but childhood is also affected by the way in which generation is viewed. Cultures vary in their response to old people, for instance, who might be held in great esteem or virtually ignored. So generation, like childhood, is not fixed but is socially constructed.

The notion of generation as a conceptual tool has become an important dimension in the sociology of childhood. Leena Alanen and Berry Mayall in particular have used generation as an analytical framework for studying childhood. They argue that generation is a relational concept, like gender, and just as women have traditionally been subordinated by issues of gender which construct them as 'other', so children are similarly positioned by generation. Children are united as a social category by their powerlessness and their contribution to society is marginalised by being cast as 'learning' or 'development'. Both Mayall and Alanen believe that knowledge of society is partial and biased if it does not include the exploration of relationships from children's perspectives and this can help redress the balance of 'adultist' sociology.

Alanen, L (1994) Gender and generation in Qvortrup, J et al (eds) *Childhood Matters*. Aldershot: Avebury

Alanen, L and Mayall, B (eds) (2001) *Conceptualising child–adult relations*. Abingdon: Routledge Falmer.

Mayall, B (2002) *Towards a sociology of childhood: thinking from children's lives*. Buckingham: Open University Press.

ACTIVITY 5

Talk to grandparents or other older people of your acquaintance.

Ask them about their experiences of schooling and of work.

At what age did they leave school? What sort of expectations did they have?

How do they feel their lives compare to those of their parents?

How does your own experience of childhood differ from that of your grandparents?

Childhood continues to evolve and change; it is a dynamic rather than a static concept and continues to change over time as society itself evolves. In this way childhood may be seen to be in a constant state of transformation or reconstruction (James and Prout, 1997).

SUMMARY

Whether or not you are convinced by Ariès and Postman's view that the concept of childhood is a modern invention, the actual experience of being a child has changed dramatically throughout history. In the past children were not separated from public life as they routinely are nowadays and the expectation would have been that they should earn their living as soon as they were able. Increasing public perception of children as a social group distinct from adults grew slowly supported by the popularity of certain writers whose ideas have continued to influence the ways in which children are understood.

The changing experience of childhood accelerated after the Industrial Revolution when concerns about child labour began to surface. Gradual social reform led eventually to universal compulsory education which changed the status of the child from wage earner to schoolchild. With this change came the idea of childhood as a time of dependency and by the twentieth century parents had begun to focus on children's psychological and emotional rather than economic value.

Childhood has always been affected by particular discourses which construct the child as inherently wicked or else naturally innocent. These contribute to an understanding of childhood which combines conflicting portrayals of children as innocent, vulnerable, dependent, incapable, incompetent and in need of protection and control as if these are all 'natural' attributes of the child.

A prolonged childhood as a stage of life determined by adult control and supervision is a modern concept. Cunningham suggests that the ingredients of the contemporary experience of childhood have been in place for about half a century only (2003, p.110). This is an important reminder that childhood remains a contestable concept which is open to debate.

FURTHER READING

Cunningham, H (1995) *Children and childhood in Western society since 1500*. London: Longman Group Ltd.

This is the most comprehensive study of the changing position of children throughout history.

Cunningham, H (2006) *The invention of childhood*. London: BBC Books.

An immensely readable account of childhood in Britain over the past 1000 years. The use of diaries and letters brings the voices of children and their parents alive to demonstrate the continuities of the experience of childhood as well as the many changes. The accompanying BBC Radio 4 series is also available on CD. (See also website below.)

Gabriel, N (2010) Adults' concepts of childhood in Parker Rees, R, Leeson, C, Willan, J and Savage, J (eds) *Early childhood studies* (3rd edition). Exeter: Learning Matters.

An interesting discussion of the ways in which adults interpret and explain childhood.

Hendrick, H (1997) Constructions and reconstructions of British childhood: an interpretive survey, 1800 to the present, in James, A, and Prout, A, (eds) *Constructing and reconstructing childhood: contemporary issues in the sociological study of childhood* (2nd edition). Lewes: Falmer Press.

Hendrick has written widely about changing conceptions of childhood and the implications of these. This chapter is a good overview of the ways in which the child has been variously understood over the past 200 years as a result of changing social circumstances.

Horn, P (1989) *The Victorian and Edwardian schoolchild*. Gloucester: Alan Sutton Publishing.

An illustrated history of the development of schooling after the Education Act of 1870 supported by many original photographs.

WEBSITES

www.open2.net/theinventionofchildhood

Developed by the Open University and the BBC this site supports Hugh Cunningham's *The Invention of Childhood* (see above) and has useful links to related topics.

3 | The context of the family

Through reading this chapter, you will:

- examine the diversity of family forms and understand the way that changes in society affect the family structure;
- consider some theoretical explanations and critiques of the family;
- examine perceptions of the breakdown of traditional families and some of the consequences of these concerns;
- understand some of the ways that the state impacts on the family and begin to recognise the underlying assumptions that affect such action.

The microsystem of the family is the social institution which most affects children's early experiences.

Introduction

Until the new social studies of childhood placed them firmly in a central position in their own right (see Introduction on page 1), children were mainly understood sociologically as units located within the social institution of the family. Such a view also dominated psychology which emphasised concepts such as 'bonding' and 'maternal deprivation' as well as social policy which focused on the family unit. All of this was based on an underlying assumption that the interests of the child and the interests of the family were one and the same thing. Despite two decades of debates which challenge this view, the concept of the family is still the prime way in which society understands childhood politically, economically and through everyday life. Daniel and Ivatts (1998) draw attention to the way we even use the term 'family' to mean 'children' in conversation – consider such phrases as 'Do you have a family?' and 'They are going to start a family'. Qvortrup (1994) calls this process the 'familialisation' of the child and argues that the child as an individual is often obscured by a focus on the family unit.

What is a family?

The family is a basic social group, generally connected by kinship or marriage, which aims to provide its members with mutual social, emotional and economic security. The structure of the family varies widely although some sort of communal living arrangement exists in all societies. The predominant family model in the West is the *nuclear family* and, for the majority of children, some variation on this is likely to form the prime microsystem (see Chapter 1) for socialisation; however, it must be remembered that not all children will live in such family units and some may not live within families at all.

Changes in society have brought about corresponding changes in the family. In particular the role of women has been transformed in recent decades. A number of things have contributed to this including the availability of contraception and legal abortion, reform of the law to make divorce more straightforward, and greater equality for women in general, including more access to higher education and, therefore, increased career aspirations. As a result women are much more likely to postpone having children until they have established a career; they can also space out pregnancies and limit the size of their families. Perhaps most importantly, they are more easily able to leave unsatisfactory marriages and have greater financial independence to enable them to do so.

ACTIVITY 1

Draw your family unit identifying siblings, parents, grandparents, aunts, uncles and cousins as well as any step-parents and half-brothers or -sisters.

Ask a grandparent to tell you about their family life when they were young. If you do not have a living grandparent, talk to another older person of your acquaintance.

Compare the differences.

The changes already identified have all had repercussions for the make-up of the modern family and this has resulted in greater recognition and acceptance of family diversity (Silva and Smart, 1999). Divorce is much more common than it used to be as well as remarriage and so there are many more lone parent families as well as 'blended' or 'reconstituted' families where children are growing up with half-siblings and step-parents (Social Trends, 2009). Whereas there was once a stigma attached to having a child outside marriage, this is no longer frowned upon and many cohabiting couples bring up happy and stable families. This has also made it easier for lone parents and so some single women choose to become mothers and bring up children on their own without the support of a father. Increased acceptance of gay lifestyles means that a number of same-sex couples have been able to start a family with the help of sperm and egg donors. Immigration and the greater cultural diversity of the UK have also had an effect on the make-up of the family. There is now a much higher number of dual-heritage children than in the past as well as extended families which include the presence of grandparents and other family members within the household; multigenerational families are particularly to be found among British citizens originating from the Asian subcontinent.

Social changes also *reduce* the prevalence of some types of family – for instance, the availability of contraception and safe and legal abortion means far fewer unwanted babies are born and available for adoption. Couples unable to have children of their own would once have been able to adopt a healthy newborn; now they are more likely to turn to in-vitro fertilisation (IVF) techniques. International adoption, where prospective parents adopt children from poorer countries, has become much more common as the supply of local babies has reduced and this receives considerable attention in the media as a result of a few high-profile celebrity adoptions.

At the beginning of the twenty-first century only 61 per cent of children in the UK actually live in a 'traditional' family with married parents although there are considerable regional variations – for instance, the percentage is higher in Northern Ireland and lower in London (Bayliss and Sly, 2009). Nonetheless, this model of family life continues to dominate public discussion of the family and is usually at the forefront of politicians' minds when formulating social policy.

Because ideas about the 'typical' child have such a strong hold on perceptions of childhood, children with disabilities challenge popular ideals of the perfect family. We have already considered how advances in medicine bring about changes to the family through reproductive technologies like contraception and IVF; this has also affected family experience of disability. Early screening techniques, along with safe and accessible abortion, mean there is often now a choice about whether or not to bring a disabled child into the world. At the same time, developments in perinatal care have increased the chance of survival for children born with a disability who would once have died. Like IVF and sperm donation, these developments raise moral and ethical dilemmas that are likely to increase in the future with new advances in technology such as stem-cell research.

At one time children with disabilities were routinely hidden away, frequently in specialist institutions, until the *Warnock Report* (DES, 1978) increased awareness of their needs. The 1981 Education Act introduced legislation to support Warnock's recommendations removing the term 'handicap' and introducing instead the concept of special educational need. In the following decades further steps have been made towards integration, and later inclusion, of children with disabilities into mainstream schooling (DfES, 2001). However, these issues continue to create controversy and although there is an increased emphasis on inclusion within policy documentation, disabled children and their families are rarely evident in the wider social sphere.

ACTIVITY 2

Over the next week research how families are depicted on television.

Pay particular attention to the make-up of the family – look for traditional, nuclear families, lone parent families, reconstituted families and any other models you can identify.

Think about the 'messages' that are conveyed by these illustrations of family life. What are the assumptions that underpin them?

Consider where these different representations are most likely to appear.

For instance, you are likely to find a quite different sort of family advertising breakfast cereal than you will find in soap operas.

Why might this be? What is the image of the family being used for?

Are there any assumptions being made about class, culture and ethnicity?

Can you find any families which have children with disabilities?

continued

ACTIVITY **2** *continued*

Are these portrayed as normal, happy families or are they presented as objects of pity, people to be admired for overcoming great difficulties or as an unusual spectacle in contrast to 'normal' family life?

What is likely to be the effect of these representations for viewers?

How might they reinforce or distort preconceptions?

How will they affect the self-image of children who come from non-traditional families?

Differing perspectives of the family

The nuclear family is often referred to as a 'traditional' family and is made up of a hetero-sexual married couple and their biological offspring. This traditional model comprises no more than two generations and includes dependent children supported by parents until they reach maturity at which time they will leave to start another nuclear family of their own. In reality only a proportion of children are growing up in such families today but this model of the family unit continues to hold a strong emotional appeal framing ideas of what the family should be – this is the reason why 'cornflake families', as they are often referred to, feature frequently in marketing and advertising. Much anxiety about family life in contemporary society comes from the idea of the breakdown of such family patterns.

One of the main reasons for the pervasiveness of the nuclear family model is due to the influence of Murdock (1968) who studied families across the world and claimed that the nuclear family was universal. Although Murdock's assumptions have since been challenged, the idea that the family performs a vital role in society is behind much of the contemporary concern about the apparent 'breakdown' of the family. From this perspective, increasing divorce rates are a dangerous trend demonstrating collapse of the traditional family and a threat to social order.

THEORY FOCUS

Functionalist views of the family

Functionalism is a key sociological concept, related to structure, which analyses the role of a social institution through the function which it performs.

Murdock's study of the family is a prime example of functionalism.

He believed that the family as an institution is important because it performs four functions essential for the successful organisation of any society:

- reproduction of the population to ensure the continuation of society;

- a location for the socialisation of the young so that children absorb the norms and values of their society;

- the provision of economic support through the division of labour;

• providing an acceptable outlet for sexual urges so that social order and public morality can be maintained.

Functionalism is now regarded as rather outdated but was very prominent in the post-war years; the influence of this ideological way of thinking about family is evident in the development of the welfare state and is an area that will be discussed further in Chapter 6.

An underpinning assumption of the functionalist perspective was that the family is a good thing which must be supported. Not everyone would agree with this viewpoint and feminists in particular have argued that the traditional family unit can disadvantage women and children (Coppock, 2004). Feminists have highlighted the unequal power relationships and division of tasks within families as well as ways in which traditional gender expectations are reproduced so that boys take on masculine traits and girls learn to be mothers. This passing on of social norms is one of the important roles of the family from a functionalist perspective, but of course this assumes agreement about which values should be reproduced. A patriarchal (male-based) model of family life means that much of the 'work' of the family, such as shopping, cooking, cleaning, laundry as well as emotional nurturing, is commonly viewed as the traditional role of women. This work is taken for granted and undervalued and is often performed on top of paid employment. Feminists have drawn attention to the way this reinforces the separation of 'public' and 'private' aspects of society and how women and children have always been identified with private family life (for example, Smart, 1984; Dobash and Dobash, 1992). The repercussions of this artificial division are widespread and range from expectations about childcare to attitudes towards domestic abuse.

THEORY FOCUS

Feminist perspectives

Feminism refers to theoretical and political perspectives which study and contest the subordinate position of women in society. Feminism challenges the *patriarchal* system – the established social, political and cultural system(s) whereby men are in a dominant position in relation to women. Feminists recognise that women and girls are disadvantaged within patriarchal society and challenge the practices, beliefs and processes based on power differentials which systematically disadvantage one gender rather than the other.

Feminism as an academic study mainly emerged in the 1970s although some important books predate this. This period is often designated 'second wave' feminism to differentiate it from suffragist campaigns for the vote early in the twentieth century. As feminism became more established a number of perspectives emerged each of which took a different approach depending on their analysis of the issues. These perspectives have different implications for early childhood practice and policy.

Liberal feminism stemming from humanitarian ideas of freedom and human rights, argues that women should have the same rights and opportunities as men. Campaigns to change

continued

practices discriminating against women have resulted in such legislation as the Equal Pay Act 1970 and the Sex Discrimination Act 1975.

Liberal feminists see problems of gender arising through socialisation of children. They claim differences in aspirations and expectations are learned as children grow up and that child-rearing practices create behaviours commonly viewed as typically female or male. This perspective has been criticised for taking social institutions like the family for granted and failing to challenge social arrangements. For instance, it is fair enough to argue that women should have career opportunities – but this is often not possible because of family responsibilities and lack of adequate childcare.

Radical feminism identified the concept of patriarchy suggesting that the problem lies in the social arrangement of gender and the gendered nature of relationships between men and women. This view suggests that women as a class or social group are oppressed by men as a class and demonstrates a different emphasis; liberal feminists emphasise human values rather than gender whereas radical feminists value femaleness itself. They believe that the important thing is not to enable women to take part in the world *as if they were men* – but to value women in their own right. The phrase 'the personal is political' comes from radical feminists who recognised that gender pervades all areas of women's lives and gender inequalities are not only located in the public sphere. Rather than trying to bring in laws and policies, radical feminism attempts to challenge gender relations and social attitudes. The main criticism of this perspective is that it appears to suggest that patriarchy is responsible for most social problems which would cease to exist if gendered relationships were different.

Marxist feminism identifies the fundamental problem not as patriarchy but as capitalism. From this viewpoint class rather than gender is seen as the most important social variable. Marxists offer economic explanations of why women have subordinate and dependent status. They argue that the economic system works only because it is held together by women who both support and reproduce workers – i.e. they care for the physical needs of the family (food, clothes, sickness) and also bear children. Women are not paid to do this work but their domestic role is essential for the continuation of capitalism, therefore Marxist feminists believe capitalism must be eradicated if women are to have equality. This perspective can be challenged because it cannot explain unequal gender relations outside capitalist systems. (See Chapter 6, page 77, for further discussion of Marxism.)

Socialist feminism considers that capitalism and patriarchy together are responsible for women's social position and tries to explain how women are brought up to desire marriage and children as their prime goal in life whereas men are expected to derive their sense of self largely from a job or career. Socialist feminism identifies social institutions, primarily the family and school, as sites where gender relations are reproduced. The education system appears to be egalitarian but because it reinforces class and gender divisions it is itself an agent of oppression. By producing large numbers of young women whose abilities and skills are less valued than those of young men, a potential reserve labour force of cheap, casual or part-time workers is created. This keeps women dependent on men and supports capitalism because female workers can be brought in to fill gaps and easily dismissed when no longer needed.

Other perspectives also exist such as black feminism, which recognises that black women can be doubly oppressed by both gender and ethnicity but this viewpoint has had much more impact in the USA than Britain. Few feminists would specifically identify themselves with one of these labels, but they are a useful tool to analyse different approaches.

Oakley (1994) and Alanen (1994) have drawn attention to ways in which both women and children were habitually marginalised within traditional explanations of society and the many similarities between theorising gender and theorising childhood.

The impact of feminism has been considerable in increasing awareness of power differentials within society and the implicit patriarchal assumptions that affect family life. However, this has not always been welcomed and feminists have come under attack from the 'New Right' who take the view that such ideas encourage women to disregard their conventional role and responsibilities, thus undermining traditional values and leading to social collapse. (The political ideologies which shape ideas about social policy are examined in Chapter 6.)

In response to the emergence of so many 'new' kinds of families, some sociologists have started to rethink the fundamental concept of the family itself. Instead of seeing it as a fixed social form, they suggest it is more helpful to consider 'family' as something that people do; an activity that can be recognised through 'family practices' (Morgan, 1996; Silva and Smart, 1999). Seen from this perspective, what it means to be a parent, a child or a sibling depends on negotiated roles and identities within the support system of a family. Wyness (2006) points out that the concept of 'doing' family challenges children's traditional role as passive dependants and makes their contribution to family life more visible.

What would you identify as examples of 'family practices'?

To what extent are these common to a variety of family forms?

What are the implications of thinking of the family as a fixed entity (i.e. as a 'thing') or, alternatively, as a human activity and something that people 'do'?

Anxieties about changing family relationships

Families were once structured around established roles and responsibilities, firmly delineated by gender and generation. Radical changes in family forms, structures and function have had a significant effect on the lives of both children and adults. While welcome to many, for some people these are disturbing changes and provoke anxiety about the 'breakdown' of the family. Much of this debate is to do with authority and power as autocratic parenting styles have changed and parents look for more friendly ways of interacting with their children. Giddens refers to this as the 'democritisation' of family and says:

> There is only one story to tell about the family today, and that is of democracy. The family is becoming democratised in ways which track processes of public democracy; and ... [d]emocracy in the public sphere involves formal equality, individual rights, public discussion of issues free from violence, and authority, which is negotiated rather than given by tradition.

(1998, p.93)

Relationships between family members nowadays are more likely to reflect the greater equality and more informal attitudes in society as a whole, both between men and women and between generations. Giddens recognises that *there can be no going back* from the principle of equality between the sexes and in reality there can be few who would wish to return to a time when fathers ruled households in which wives and children were subservient. One of the major impacts of changing gender relationships within the family has been a different role for men as fathers want more involvement in their children's lives. Indeed, expectations of the role of fathers have changed so much that now a major concern is that fathers do not spend enough time with their children. Sue Palmer recently suggested that young boys are more likely to become attached to TV characters such as Bob the Builder than their own fathers, warning that children could suffer emotional problems in later life (*Daily Telegraph*, 2009). This same worry was raised in the 1950s in terms of mothers' need to bond with their infants. At that time it was often taken for granted that many fathers would be a remote presence in their children's lives. This kind of contrast demonstrates how expectations of families and what it means to be a parent change over time.

THEORY FOCUS

The social impact of attachment theory

Theories do not exist in an abstract vacuum: they have real effects on real people. The impact of John Bowlby's theories about attachment and maternal deprivation is a good example of this.

Bowlby was a psychiatrist and psychoanalyst from the Tavistock Clinic studying delinquent children and the effects of institutionalised care in the 1940s. After the Second World War, the World Health Organisation commissioned Bowlby to write a report on children made homeless by the conflict. He suggested that early bonding was crucial to the child's well-being and that if children experienced 'maternal deprivation' then it was likely to create emotional and social problems in later life. Later Bowlby went on to develop his ideas into a theory of 'attachment' and it is this, rather than his maternal deprivation thesis, for which he is generally remembered today. His insights about attachment and the need for sensitive and responsive carers were enormously influential in the 1950s and were instrumental in changing the situation for young children in hospitals by enabling parental visiting and also improving conditions for children cared for by the state. However, his views have often been oversimplified or misrepresented as was the case with the closure of nurseries for working mothers in the years following the Second World War.

During both world wars, while men were away fighting, women had been called upon to take their place in factories, on the railways and buses, and in many other areas of life previously exclusively male. Many day nurseries were opened to support these female workers and the idea was encouraged that children's development would benefit from attending nursery rather than staying at home with their mother. When the soldiers returned expecting to take up their previous jobs, the idea that a woman's role was in the home and that her constant care and attention was essential to children's mental health found national favour. In 1945 the Ministry of Health issued a circular which recommended that mothers of children under two should be discouraged from working. At the same time responsibility for day nurseries was passed from national to local government and funding cut by 50 per cent (Baldock et al., 2009). Bowlby's findings were not the direct cause of this change of policy towards childcare – it was rather that they struck a chord with the feelings of the time. Therefore it is possible to see how his work formed a convenient justification for the closure of hundreds of workplace nurseries that had opened during the war years.

Bowlby's views have been challenged by many people, primarily Michael Rutter (1981). It is now generally accepted that the bonding and affection important to an infant's emotional well-being is likely to come from several sources. Nonetheless Bowlby's views continue to have a powerful effect on ideas about childcare; their influence can be seen, for instance, in the extension of parental leave and development of the Key Person role in the Early Years Foundation Stage (DfES, 2007). The modern concept of 'quality time' might also be seen as an aspect of anxiety and guilt from working parents about leaving their children in the care of others.

Although Palmer (*Daily Telegraph*, 2009) identifies fathers as too busy to bond with their children, increasingly this is a concern of mothers too as working women become the norm rather than an exception. However, this is a misconception arising from an increasing emphasis on 'quality time' and the subsequent anxiety parents feel about the emotional well-being of their offspring. Today's parents, although working, actually spend *more* time with their children than any previous generation – an average of 99 minutes a day rather than the 25 minutes a day averaged in 1975 (Future Foundation, 2006). What has actually changed is the social *expectation* of parenting as the idea took hold that spending time playing with one's children is valuable and important.

Another anxiety about modern families is concern about single parents. Despite the widespread view that lone parent families are a modern phenomenon, there were in reality just as many 'broken' and 'reconstituted' families in the past (Cunningham, 2006) – the difference being that these usually came about as the result of early death rather than divorce. Historical evidence suggests that, despite contemporary misgivings, the twentieth century was actually more 'conforming and stable' in terms of family life than any previous period (Anderson,1995, cited in Coppock, 2004). Before the welfare state and greater employment opportunities, women were dependent on men, leaving those who were widowed or abandoned to be pitied and in need of charity. However, nowadays the benefit system enables women to make independent choices and to look after their children without the support of men. Thus they can be viewed as a threat to 'normal' social order and 'traditional family values'. All political parties are eager not to be seen to encourage 'welfare dependency' and so social policies frequently penalise non-traditional family structures. As a result, lone parents and their children are more likely to suffer high levels of poverty; a situation which is not helped by largely incorrect and damaging stereotypes.

One of the effects of changing family structures is that many young parents no longer have extended family living close to whom they can turn for help and support. In recent years an entire parenting 'industry' (Guldberg, 2009) has developed to fill this gap with books, websites and television programmes offering advice. Of course there have always been books written about the upbringing of children (both Locke and Rousseau were 'best-sellers' in their day – see Chapter 2, page 21), but the sheer proliferation of advice nowadays can actually serve to undermine and decrease parents' confidence in their ability to look after their own children. Television programmes such as *Supernanny* give the impression that children are very difficult to manage and have given rise to a level of anxiety that has been termed 'paranoid' (Furedi, 2001). Guldberg argues that this contemporary preoccupation does more harm than good:

> ... *undermining parents' common sense, which has been quite good enough for generations, is more likely to damage parent child relationships ... The more parents are led to believe that they are likely to mess up unless they seek expert advice the more stilted and insecure they are likely to become in the way they relate to their children.*
>
> (2009, p.146)

Lewis has shown that anxieties about the family are common at times of military or economic crisis (1986). She claims that social upheaval frequently results in widespread concern about the perceived 'failure' of the family although this will take different forms at different historical periods. In this way, concern about the family might be seen to parallel the widespread anxieties about childhood itself which are explored in Chapter 9. Worries about the 'breakdown' of family life therefore need to be seen within a context of the restructuring of modern life and the great changes in material and economic circumstances brought about by advanced capitalism (Coppock, 2004).

The family in public policy

Feminist analyses of the family show that the relationship between the state and the family is not neutral but underpinned by ideological assumptions about the roles of women and children. For instance, changes from the traditional patriarchal family in which the father was the breadwinner and the mother took sole responsibility for care of the children have caused tensions for working women who are now frequently torn between their family and their career. Similarly notions that the child's rightful place is within the family shape how public policy is formulated; for example, children are now placed with foster parents wherever possible rather than in children's homes. The 1989 Children Act was built on the assumption that children are best looked after in families, so that the focus changed from removing children from 'dysfunctional' families to supporting families to look after their children more effectively.

This Act replaced the legal principle of parents' rights with that of parental responsibility and was the beginning of a much stronger emphasis on partnership with the family, further reinforced by the subsequent Children Act of 2004. Traditionally, in the UK, there has been a habit of viewing the family as a private institution which the state should not interfere with unless necessary (Archard, 1993). Unlike some other countries such as France and Scandinavia where there is a much greater emphasis on public responsibility for children, in Britain children have customarily been viewed as a 'private indulgence rather than a public responsibility' (Daniel and Ivatts, 1998). As a result, public policy towards children developed from the view that responsibility for the care and welfare of children was a private matter and outside the scope of government. State intervention was only considered appropriate when children were in actual danger. Although the Children Act of 1989 is usually seen as a landmark in legislation for children, Gary Walker (2008) points out the importance of recognising its political context. Passed at a time when the New Right government of the day emphasised minimal state intervention, the state's attitude towards families is evident in the notion that children are effectively the private property of their parents. This debate about the limits, boundaries and overlap between private responsibility and public intervention is an ongoing one and is considered in more detail in connection with models of social welfare in Chapter 6.

The underlying philosophy of public policy with regard to children has shifted in recent years to a recognition that all kinds of families are likely to benefit from support in bringing up their children at some point. Recently the introduction to the Children's Plan has made this intention explicit:

> *Parents bring up children, not government, but parents need help and support to do their job.*

> (DCSF, 2007, p.1)

As a result, greater emphasis on working in partnership with parents can be identified throughout government policy (and is discussed further in Chapter 4). Reinforced by the Every Child Matters agenda, this affects all areas of children's lives and has been strengthened by the creation of a new government department, the Department for Children, Schools and Families, to combine governance and bring together professionals and agencies working with children and their families. Such a family focus dominates both practice and policy and it has been claimed that professional training and practice is now frequently framed in terms of the family rather than being child-centred (Tomlinson, 2008). It is dangerous to assume that the child's interests and the interests of the family are necessarily the same thing. Children's own interests can often be overlooked unless children are valued and respected as people with rights and identities of their own.

One of the reasons for a growing focus on the family is the belief that preventative measures in the Early Years can save problems (and money) later on; parenting is increasingly being viewed as a way of countering any number of social ills (Aitken and Jones,

2005). In developing the Children's Plan in response to widespread concern regarding the well-being of British children, the government made a large investment in family workers to provide targeted support to struggling families. The Common Assessment Framework (CAF) sets out dimensions of 'parenting capacity' in terms of providing basic care, ensuring safety and protection, emotional warmth, stability, guidance, boundaries and stimulation. However, some commentators are concerned that such actions are built on a discourse of an 'ideal' family (Scraton, 2004; Aitken and Jones, 2005) and are primarily concerned with regulating families and imposing middle-class values. These ideas are explored further in Chapter 5 in connection with Sure Start.

Although most public policy talks of partnership with parents, in reality social expectations which construct women as the prime care givers mean that mothers bear the brunt of initiatives to promote good parenting. In recent years there have been a number of moves to engage with fathers but as Leverett (2008a) points out, the involvement of fathers is still far behind, particularly if they are young or from an ethnic minority background.

ACTIVITY 4

Look online at any recent legislation and policy initiatives such as the Children Act 2004, Every Child Matters, the Early Years Foundation Stage and the Children's Plan to pick out what is stated about parents and families.

What are the underlying values and expectations that are implicit in these documents?

Do you feel that these apply to all families or do they favour white middle-class parenting styles?

It is important to bear in mind that what is best for parents or the family as a whole is not necessarily the same as the best interests of the child.

Can you identify any potential areas of conflict?

What difficulties could these raise for professionals working with children and their families?

SUMMARY

Rapid social changes of many kinds over the past few decades have brought about corresponding changes in family structure and this has led to widespread anxiety about the collapse of family life. Although Bernardes has suggested that '...the nuclear family does not exist except as a powerful image in the mind' (1997, p.13), in practice this model of the traditional family is extremely influential in regulating national policy as well as shaping professional practice in the field. Theoretical explanations of the family can help us to analyse different perspectives but public policy in respect of the family is ultimately determined by political ideology and beliefs about what the family ought to be. In this way, national legislation and social policy frameworks play a considerable role in reinforcing expectations about family relationships and responsibilities. However, the fact that children are more often identified as members of a family rather than as separate

SUMMARY *continued*

individuals can make them socially 'invisible' and as a result social policy is less likely to be developed specifically around their needs (Daniel and Ivatts, 1998).

For many years the family was considered as a purely private affair in which the state should not interfere except in exceptional circumstances. However, recent policy initiatives, in particular Every Child Matters, are built upon the idea that families and professionals should work in partnership to meet the needs of the child. Consequently it is important that the interests of the child are not overlooked as a result of an increasing focus on the family. Concerns have also been raised that the move to work more closely with parents is in reality a way of imposing middle-class values on families that do not conform to prevailing ideologies.

FURTHER READING

Aitken, S and Jones, L (2005) Exploring families, in Jones, L, Holmes, R and Powell, J (eds) *Early childhood studies: a multiprofessional perspective*. Maidenhead: Open University Press/McGraw-Hill Education.

An interesting deconstruction of 'the family' that will help you question the way families are understood and the discourses that create and support these perspectives.

Archard, D (2003) *Children, family and the state*. Aldershot: Ashgate Publishing.

A clear discussion of the complex issue of rights and relationships between the child, the family and the state.

Coppock, V (2004) 'Families' in 'crisis'? in Scraton, P (ed) *'Childhood' in 'crisis'?* Abingdon: Routledge.

This chapter provides a thorough discussion about historical and theoretical perspectives of the family and considers the political dimensions of the family.

Silva, EB and Smart, C (1999) *The new family*. London: Sage.

A helpful account of changing family structures and the place of the family within contemporary society.

WEBSITES

www.statistics.gov.uk/socialtrends39/
Social trends website focusing on statistics for families and children in 2009 – the last year for which statistics were available at the time of writing.

www.familyandparenting.org/
Website of the Family and Parenting Institute, a research and policy unit that is a central source for information, research and resources to do with families.

www.dcsf.gov.uk/childrensplan/
Government portal related to the Children's Plan which gives access to a wide range of information, advice and resources about families and provides links to a number of other useful sites.

www.nationalstrategies.standards.dcsf.gov.uk/primary/features/foundation_stage/parents_partners/
Information about the government's Parents as Partners strategy.

4 The context of the setting

Through reading this chapter, you will:

- consider the concept of quality and how it relates to good practice;
- examine ideas about curriculum and different curricular approaches;
- understand the impact of highly trained staff;
- recognise the implications of partnership with parents;
- consider the challenges raised by multi-agency working;
- develop your awareness of issues surrounding inclusion.

Settings such as nurseries and schools are increasingly becoming an additional microsystem where children spend a large proportion of their early years.

The context of Early Years settings has changed dramatically over the past two decades and with it the role of the Early Years practitioner. Growing recognition of the importance of this role has developed alongside increased expectations of the benefits of early intervention. Early Years professionals are often looked to as having a preventative role and potential for impact in relation to every kind of social concern, from obesity to crime, child abuse to educational achievement. Peter Moss (2009) has argued that growing global interest in the Early Years stems from a belief in the child 'as a redemptive agent' and a view of childhood institutions as places where intervention can produce predetermined outcomes, thereby providing solutions to economic and social problems.

What are Early Years settings for?

In the recent past most children attended some kind of setting on a part-time basis because parents wanted their children to socialise, learn to share and prepare for school. Government policy since the 1990s, encouraging parents into work, has changed the context so that childcare has become both a necessity and a part of the economy (this issue is developed further in Chapter 6).

Economic imperatives might, therefore, suggest that the purpose of childhood institutions is to sustain an adult agenda. However, early childhood education and care (ECEC) has long been believed to benefit children themselves, although hard evidence of this was lacking until recently. Now research from the Effective Provision of Pre-school Education (EPPE) project has demonstrated how quality Early Years settings can support children's social and cognitive development (Sylva et al., 2004). The EPPE project was designed to identify factors which make Early Years settings particularly effective and has been very influential in shaping policy and practice. Its impact can be discerned in initiatives such as the Ten Year Strategy (HMT, 2004), the Early Years Foundation Stage (EYFS) (DfES, 2007) and standards for Early Years Professionals (EYPs) (CWDC, 2009).

As Early Years settings may serve a number of purposes, their effectiveness can be defined from a range of perspectives. This chapter examines the setting as it affects provision and practice; ECEC as a national social policy to support parents is considered in Chapter 6. Sylva and Taylor suggest that settings *are considered effective if children thrive in them* (2006, p.165), in other words if children make greater progress than might otherwise be expected given their backgrounds and neighbourhood. The EPPE project investigated specific features of such settings to identify which characteristics are likely to denote high quality practice. The main findings indicated that outcomes for children are improved when they attend integrated settings, led by graduate staff who support and extend thinking processes and take a balanced approach to education and social development.

THEORY FOCUS

Quality

Although quality is a term that is used recurrently in relation to ECEC it is a very difficult concept to define. Quality is a culturally-specific, value-laden idea which varies over time and place (Dahlberg et al., 1999).

An increasing concern to define and measure quality has come about through growing accountability and the need to justify government expenditure. This has led to a range of different measurements and quality frameworks. For instance, the Effective Early Learning Project (EEL) identified ten different quality measures (Pascal and Bertram, 1997) to underpin quality enhancement in individual settings. Munton et al. (1995) differentiate between measures of *structure* (such as staffing and aspects of the environment) and *processes* (such as routines and interactions). The quality framework used by the EPPE research project was a development of the Early Childhood Environment Ratings Scale (ECERS) (Harms et al.,1998). While including structural aspects, this scale particularly focuses on less easily measurable process elements (Sylva, 2010).

An alternative perspective on quality is that of Katz (1993) who recognises that different stakeholders are likely to hold different views. She talks in terms of 'insiders' and 'outsiders' as well as top-down and bottom-up perspectives acknowledging that children, parents, staff, inspectors and researchers all have varying ideas about what constitutes a quality environment. This demonstrates the two main perspectives on quality – the idea that there can be objective, measurable quality indicators or alternatively that quality is relative and culturally dependent. Siraj-Blatchford and Wong argue that this polarisation is unhelpful; in their view *[t]he instruments that we apply in evaluating quality should be continually reviewed and moderated in the light of experience and developing understanding* (1999, p.17).

The culturally variable nature of quality highlights the fact that what is valued in one context may be very different to expectations elsewhere. For this reason it is inappropriate to try to apply quality indicators derived from Western practice as if they are universal measures. The increasing globalisation of childhood, considered in Chapter 7, can make this a particular

continued

THEORY FOCUS continued

danger. However, Woodhead argues that although *quality is relative, it is not arbitrary* (1998, p.7) – in other words, while recognising that ideas of quality are dependent on beliefs and values, there are still boundaries to what can be considered adequate.

For a helpful examination of issues and dilemmas around quality see:

Dahlberg, G, Moss, P and Pence, A (2007) *Beyond quality in early childhood education and care: postmodern perspectives.* 2nd edition. Abingdon: RoutledgeFalmer.

The dramatic increase in Early Years provision, particularly within the private sector, has raised concerns that quality is likely to be threatened by market forces (Penn, 2007). Ways in which the government has sought to address this are through a focus on practice (for example, the introduction of the EYFS) and staffing and by bringing Early Years settings under a regulatory framework overseen by Ofsted.

ACTIVITY **1**

To what extent can quality be measured?

Consider what different aspects of practice might be considered as quality characteristics.

Siraj-Blatchford and Wong (1999) suggest that while what *children learn may vary, how they learn it can be assessed through a common set of broadly defined but objective criteria, such as involvement and engagement.*

Do you agree with this argument? Give your reasons.

What are the implications of the 'quality dilemma' for practitioners?

Curriculum approaches

Curriculum is sometimes thought of simply in terms of content, as meaning 'what children learn' but it is important to recognise that the term denotes much more than this. The curriculum includes everything that children experience in a setting, including the routines, the ways in which resources and time are organised and the attitudes and values of the adults who they are in contact with. Although Early Years practitioners work within social and political contexts which shape the curriculum, there is still considerable autonomy in interpretation. From this perspective it is more useful to think of curriculum in terms of a dynamic process rather than as expectations to be met. Recognising the commitment this requires, MacNaughton describes curriculum as:

> a politically engaged process in which the educator's intentions and the children's involvement interact to produce the lived curriculum ...

(2003, p.113)

MacNaughton identifies three positions on the curriculum which she refers to as *conforming, reforming* and *transforming*. Each of these stems from particular beliefs about the child and the purpose of education and in turn determines the role of the educator. The *conforming* curriculum is concerned with preparing children for adult life. Therefore the emphasis is on educators passing on knowledge deemed necessary to be able to contribute to society in the future. There is also a focus on preventing unwanted behaviour. A *reforming* curriculum is based on measures which can help to develop rational and independent thinkers. Therefore the educator's role is to help children realise their potential by supporting individual interests and active involvement. There are many different ways in which such intentions might be realised and Montessori, High/Scope, Te Whãriki and Reggio Emilia approaches could all be seen as examples of this curricular position. The *transforming* curriculum is one in which education is recognised as having the potential to transform society by challenging the social order and structural inequalities such as class, race and gender. Within this position the educator's role is to challenge discrimination and oppression so as to bring about a more just and equitable society (Derman-Sparks, 1989). By recognising Maori children's rights and deliberately focusing on culture, language and community, the New Zealand Early Years curriculum, Te Whãriki, might also be considered to take a transformative position.

It is evident that an Early Years Professional accountable for high quality practice must reflect on curricular approaches in order to develop a principled stance.

ACTIVITY **2**

Research alternative approaches to the curriculum such as might be found in Montessori, Reggio Emilia, Te Whãriki and High/Scope settings.

Identify the key principles which underpin these perspectives.

Consider how time, space and material resources are organised within these approaches.

How might your own practice benefit from examining alternative curricular models?

The development of a curriculum for the Early Years

Bennett (2003) identifies two underlying approaches to the curriculum; one being the social pedagogic style common in Scandinavia and the other a pre-school approach which focuses on preparing children for formal education. Although the curricular frameworks which underpin provision in the UK seek to integrate care and education and promote play-based active learning, the underlying philosophy remains this pre-school approach. The emphasis on educational standards, literacy and numeracy within the National Curriculum exerts a powerful push downwards.

The curriculum for under-fives has gradually evolved since the late 1990s. Until the Desirable Outcomes (DLOs) (DfEE/SCAA, 1996) there were no curriculum guidelines for the pre-school age group, although there was general agreement among practitioners that good practice required a broad, balanced range of active, hands-on experiences to support holistic development (Dowling, 1992; Curtis, 1998). The DLOs were introduced largely for political and organisational ends; their failure to consider play and the emphasis on 'outcomes' and preparation for school made them deeply unpopular. They were later replaced by the Curriculum Guidance for the Foundation Stage (CGFS) (QCA/ DfEE, 2000) which used 'stepping stones' rather than outcomes. This helped establish formal recognition of a child's pre-school experience as important in its own right rather than simply grounding for formal schooling.

Provision for the under-threes, not covered by the CGFS, remained poor, however, until the publication of *Birth to Three Matters* (Sure Start, 2002). Although there was initially some concern that this might be a 'curriculum for babies', in fact the document was warmly received by practitioners who welcomed recognition of the importance of this age group. The framework took into account the developmental needs of very young children, for instance, by promoting the concept of key workers and emphasising the significance of relationships.

Such a 'principled' approach contrasted with the CGFS which focused instead on children's achievements and this created concerns about continuity between the two stages. Therefore, one of the aims of the Ten Year Strategy was to develop a single framework from 0–5 years. The result was the EYFS (DfES, 2007) which brought together Birth to Three Matters, the Curriculum Guidance for the Foundation Stage and the National Standards for day care and childminding, integrating both care and education within a play-based approach. The EYFS became mandatory in September 2008 and was a significant step in establishing continuity for children across different types of provision.

The development of an Early Years curriculum has occurred broadly in parallel with a move towards devolution in the UK. While the EYFS applies only to England, each of the four nations of the UK have developed their own guidance for the Early Years. The Welsh *Foundation Phase* (DCELLS, 2008) covers children from three to seven while in Scotland *A Curriculum For Excellence 3–18* (CRPB, 2006) is supplemented by *Birth to Three: Supporting our Youngest Children.* Similar developments have taken place in Northern Ireland with an enriched curriculum for younger children as well as in the Republic of Ireland, although there is still very limited state provision for the under-threes in the Republic compared to the UK (Donnelly, 2007).

The poet Yeats suggested that *education is not the filling of a pail, but the lighting of a fire* and this idea is particularly important in the contemporary world where change happens so fast. We can no longer expect to equip children with all the knowledge they will require for their future lives; instead it is important that the curriculum enables children to develop flexible and inquiring minds, and the ability to be adaptable and to think creatively. Therefore the emphasis of the curriculum has moved away from a narrow subject-based focus to an approach intended to help children develop positive learning dispositions and skills such as collaboration and problem solving. The content of the curriculum should be shaped by children's needs and interests and so the concept of an 'emergent curriculum' has arisen.

The high-quality learning experiences and interactions envisaged in the EYFS are dependent on skilled and knowledgeable practitioners who can take a personalised approach which matches the curriculum to the child, rather than the other way round, placing the child at the heart of the curriculum.

The workforce

The National Childcare Strategy launched in 1998 was intended to address the legacy of neglect of the Early Years sector, evident in fragmented services and a poorly trained workforce with limited access to training or opportunities for progression. A confusing number of different qualifications from a range of different sources existed so the Qualifications and Curriculum Authority (QCA) was charged with developing a coherent framework of Early Years qualifications. A Common Core of Skills and Knowledge for the Children's Workforce (DfES, 2005) and an Integrated Qualifications Framework (IQF) should enable mobility, progression and shared values across services.

The issue of training and qualifications is particularly significant because, historically, Early Years settings have been staffed by a predominantly low-skilled female workforce, the majority of whom have qualifications at level 3 or below. This is especially the case in the private sector where there is a very high turnover of staff and limited opportunities for continuing professional development (CPD). Baldock et al. (2009) suggest that because childcare has traditionally been seen as a service for parents, the government does not step in to subsidise settings and ensure investment in high-quality staff, in contrast to other European countries where childcare is seen as a service to children themselves. They estimate that only 3 per cent of practitioners in private settings are graduates compared to 40 per cent in maintained settings. The main reason for this disparity has been a persistent split between education and care, identified by Bennett (2003) as one of the most important issues facing ECEC within the UK and beyond. Education has traditionally been viewed as superior to the care sector which had a perceived lower status. A large proportion of training within the care sector has been provided through NVQs which carry a danger of simply *recycling bad practice* (Jackson and Fawcett, 2009, p.129).

A more encouraging prospect is emerging as a consequence of the EPPE report which clearly demonstrated the impact of highly trained professionals on the quality of settings (Sylva et al., 2010). Outcomes for children's development and learning dispositions have been shown to be measurably better in learning environments where staff value and extend children's thought processes. Settings which employ staff with higher qualifications are more likely to foster this sustained shared thinking through joint involvement and investigations. Evidence from EPPE informed the government's Ten Year Strategy, one of the objectives of which was to develop a world class workforce. This was reinforced in the Children's Plan (DCSF, 2007) and lay behind recent moves to enhance quality through the Graduate Leader Fund (DCSF, 2008) to support professional development of staff. Recognition of the importance of the practitioner's role through the introduction of Early Years Professional Status (EYPS) has been an important move in professionalising the workforce and enhancing the status of the sector (McDowall Clark and Baylis, 2010). The role of the EYP and their relationship with teachers and other professionals is still evolving but it is evident that Early Years settings will require expert pedagogues similar to those found in many other European countries. The management and leadership of integrated centres also requires specialist skills and knowledge, recognised in the development of the National Professional Qualification in Integrated Centre Leadership (NPQICL).

The Children's Workforce Development Council (CWDC), set up in 2005, has been instrumental in these moves to reform and upskill the workforce, promote interagency working and develop a common culture. Although CWDC only concerns the workforce in England, comparable bodies are similarly engaged in other parts of the UK. It is evident that, as well as lacking higher level qualifications, the staff in Early Years settings are not representative of the population as a whole and therefore of the children and families with whom they work. Baldock et al. (2009) claim that more than a third are below the age of 25, that 99 per cent are female and that there are few disabled practitioners or those from minority cultural backgrounds. The current situation poses a number of challenges but Clark and Waller (2007) are concerned that an emphasis on structural change can hide the extent to which cultural change is also necessary.

ACTIVITY 3

Consider the workforce in any setting(s) you are familiar with.

To what extent are staff representative of the families they support?

Discuss with your peers the advantages of a more diverse workforce.

What barriers prevent a greater proportion of people from different cultural backgrounds from joining the profession?

How might you encourage more male workers and practitioners with a disability?

One of the greatest challenges facing the Early Years sector is sustainability and affordability (Pugh, 2010). While the government set a target of one graduate in every setting by 2015, with two in the 30 per cent most disadvantaged areas, there is a need for a definite career framework, opportunities for CPD and clear progression routes if such professionals are to be recruited and retained in the field. Pay levels within the private, voluntary and independent (PVI) sector are a major concern and although the Ten Year Strategy suggested that *[w]orking with pre-school children should have as much status as a profession as teaching children in schools* (HMT, 2004, p.44), pay remains a serious stumbling block to achieving this. A commitment to investment in CPD and master's qualifications for teachers spelled out in the Ten Year Strategy and the Children's Plan also suggests that the differential in status between teachers and EYPs could remain for the foreseeable future (McDowall Clark and Hanson, 2007).

Working in partnership with parents and colleagues

Partnership working, both with parents and other professionals, is nowadays considered fundamental to good practice and is underpinned by the Children Act 2004 (DfES, 2004b).

However Aubrey (2010) suggests that partnership as a concept is poorly defined and is applied to a range of diverse practices. Partnership refers to the strategic frameworks through which services are delivered as well as to a style of working. In relation to working with parents, although there is no doubt about the good intentions of practitioners and policy makers, the reality may be very different. Lamb (cited in Penn, 2004) points out how the literature about child development is built on an assumption that the white middle classes have superior parenting skills. Therefore 'working with families' may be primarily concerned with reinforcing particular practices and directed predominantly at ethnic minority families and children from poor working-class backgrounds. James and James (2004) suggest that collaboration with parents is often an attempt at recruiting them as partners in 'controlling' children to make them conform to expectations. The way in which assumptions about families underpin policy is discussed in Chapter 3.

Partnerships with parents are also likely to take different forms dependent on practitioners' ideas of the curriculum discussed above. MacNaughton (2003) suggests that within conforming approaches, practitioners are viewed as possessing expertise and frequently dismiss parents' and carers' knowledge as 'anecdotal' and inadequate. There is often an emphasis on teaching parents the appropriate ways to interact with their children. Under such circumstances it is not surprising that some parents may resist moves towards 'parental involvement', even at the risk of being labelled poor parents uninterested in their children's well-being. MacNaughton warns that:

> When early childhood educators subordinate parents' knowledge to their own, they create hierarchical relationships with parents that make it hard to communicate with them equitably, especially with parents whose ways of behaving with children they regard as inappropriate.
>
> (2003, p.261)

Leverett (2008a) suggests that the Common Assessment Framework uses a broader ecological context to set out new frameworks of parenting capacity in which parents can be located without discrimination. However, establishing truly equitable and collaborative relationships requires the determination to confront power differentials which can be a challenge to the professional identity of practitioners.

Teamwork and integrated working

Threats to professional identity may also make interprofessional partnerships difficult. Integrated working was a key principle of the Every Child Matters agenda and there is an expectation that everyone working with children and families should co-operate to meet the best interests of the child. However, the reality on the ground is very variable and Aubrey (2010) warns that we should not underestimate the challenges that this can involve. The exchange of information is essential if collaboration is to be successful but this is beset by concerns about confidentiality, professional codes and ethics as well as different organisational policies and procedures. Communication difficulties may arise from different professional backgrounds and understandings. To develop successful joint working arrangements requires commitment and a willingness to put aside any rivalry over professional status. This can be difficult for some and Sanders (2009) points out how collective decision-taking runs the risk of making professionals feel deskilled.

Different ways of working in partnership

Every Child Matters: Change for Children refers to *the integration of front line delivery and the processes that support it* (DfES, 2004a, p.4). This recognises that integrated working requires a co-ordinated approach and joint working arrangements at all levels – it is not just the responsibility of practitioners working directly with children and families. At local government level Children's Trusts have been set up as partnerships of different agencies to work together and support front line practitioners. However, there are a number of terms in use in regard to integrated working which can lead to confusion. Each of these has a different focus and emphasis depending on the organisational processes involved.

Interprofessional working refers to work across different professional groups, such as an EYP supporting new mothers in partnership with a Health Visitor. However, Stone and Rixon (2008) draw attention to the difficulties this term raises because of the diversity of the children's workforce. They point out that it may marginalise those such as teaching assistants, childminders and foster carers who work in a professional capacity and have a great impact on a child's well-being in roles not usually regarded as 'professions'.

Multiprofessional means a range of professionals working together – for instance in a Children's Centre there is likely to be a team made up of family support workers, Early Years workers, a speech and language therapist, health professionals and others.

Interagency or *multi-agency* working is when different agencies work together for specific projects or to deliver particular services. Sure Start schemes or child protection conferences are both examples of partnerships which collaborate across different agencies or require joint working arrangements. Multi-agency might imply that different agencies are involved but not necessarily working in partnership whereas interagency means a joint approach.

Multidisciplinary refers to different professional backgrounds – for instance, health workers have been trained in a scientific, medical discipline which is built on quite different values and principles to those of social workers who come from a social science background. Such differences may be 'invisible' to practitioners who take their own understanding of issues for granted and so could get in the way of interprofessional or interagency communication if they are not carefully examined and shared.

Although effective integrated working is not easy to achieve, there are many benefits to children and families. Services are more likely to meet a child's needs through co-ordinated action because expertise can be shared. Service users are saved from the confusion of accessing a large number of different professionals and agencies, and multiple assessments of a child can be avoided. Integrated working should also enable more effective use of resources so that a better quality of service may be delivered at less cost.

Children with complex needs are likely to interact with a bewildering array of different professionals and agencies but many families are likely to have periods in their life when they need additional help from outside sources. Discuss the following case study with your peers.

Amy is three years old. She has a hearing loss which has slowed her language development although otherwise her progress appears to be typical. Amy's mother recently gave birth to a new baby and the Health Visitor is concerned that she appears to be exhibiting signs of post-natal depression. Amy attends private day care three days a week and had settled well although Nicky, her key person, is worried her behaviour has deteriorated over the last two months. Nicky is unsure whether this is due to changed circumstances in the home or is rooted in Amy's language delay which increasingly impedes her play with other children as the difference in their ability to communicate becomes more marked.

How many different professionals might be involved with Amy?

How could better co-ordination simplify processes?

Communication across different agencies can also be difficult because the professional terminology used to support practice may appear as jargon to those outside. Lord Laming called for *a common language for use across all agencies* (Laming, 2003, p.366). The Common Assessment Framework, (CAF), (CWDC, 2007) is intended to enable this communication and information sharing to happen in England while other countries in the UK are developing their own versions. CAF is intended for when children are not making the expected progress but the reasons why are not clear and so the involvement of other agencies is likely to be necessary. A lead professional is appointed to co-ordinate action and act as a single point of contact for the family. The intention is to enable early intervention although Jones and Leverett (2008) point out that the concept of additional needs could have a negative impact on how children view themselves and are viewed by others.

Integrated working involves more than just shared working practices and represents a different perspective of the child. In his report on the death of Victoria Climbié, Lord Laming pointed out that of all the many professionals working on the case, few saw Victoria as the central client or spoke to her directly. The key principle of integrated working should be that practitioners are outcome-focused with the child at the centre of the process rather than being service-led. Bronfenbrenner (1979) used the term mesosystem to describe the relationships between the different microsystems which the child experiences. He believed that the stronger the mesosystem was then the smoother would be children's transitions between different microsystems and the more they would thrive.

Inclusion

An active move towards recognition of children's right to inclusion can be identified in the 1989 Children Act (DoH,1989). This legislation, influenced by the United Nations

Convention on the Rights of the Child, specifically acknowledged children's right to have their identity recognised and valued. This marked a new direction in accountability for children, embracing a culture of inclusion and the reduction of discrimination. Increasing participation, the celebration of diversity and removing the barriers related to sexism, racism and perceptions of disability were intended to bring about a culture of social justice within Early Years settings. However, Nutbrown and Clough (2006) suggest that too many practitioners still regard inclusion as only being about catering for special needs. Such an attitude suggests a focus on the majority as if all children can be treated the same, regarding those who diverge from the norm in any way as a problem. A more equitable and just approach is apparent in the EYFS principle of the *Unique Child* which advocates treating each child as an individual, valuing their background, their culture and their own specific abilities.

A fully inclusive approach is about more than ensuring individual children are not disadvantaged; it also involves sensitively supporting children to make sense of difference and valuing how diversity enriches society. The main barrier to inclusion lies in people's attitudes and expectations and many factors, ranging from over-dependence on developmental charts to mistrust of unfamiliar family practices, can lead to an ethos which treats difference as a problem. In relation to culture this attitude is called *ethnocentrism* and refers to a mistrust of others and the inability to recognise the equal worth or validity of different cultural groups. Tokenistic multicultural practice may still exist alongside an ethnocentric belief that one's own group is more significant or culturally superior to other groups. Practitioners need to challenge stereotypes through an inclusive approach rather than paying lip service to equality through a few additional activities. Derman-Sparks warns against:

> the 'tourist curriculum' in which children 'visit' non-white culture and then 'go home' to the daily classroom which reflects only the dominant culture.

> (1989, p.7)

A new Single Equality Bill, introduced in the House of Commons in April 2009, is intended to bring together all the legal protection previously covered by a range of separate acts and provide protection from discrimination on the grounds of age, disability, gender, race, religion and sexual orientation. This move could help focus attention on inclusion as a right as well as recognition that genuine inclusion requires deliberate and committed action.

THEORY FOCUS

Models of disability

The way in which disability is viewed affects how people relate to children with disabilities, the expectations they hold for them, the provision available and, of course, the child's own self-image.

The *medical model* views disability as a medical problem and something that is 'wrong' with the child. This locates the disability within the child themselves and places responsibility for dealing with any problems on doctors and other health professionals.

THEORY FOCUS *continued*

In contrast, a *social model* of disability locates any problem within society, recognising that it is social structures and discriminatory attitudes which 'handicap' children with disabilities. For instance, someone with a visual impairment might require larger print or Braille to enable them to access materials alongside their sighted peers. Similarly it is the steps outside a building which prevent wheelchair users from gaining access rather than their disability. This perspective recognises that responsibility for responding to disabilities rests with everybody.

The difference in focus between these two models means that while the first identifies a deficit in the *child*, the second considers the deficit within *society* which hinders the child's inclusion.

A play-based approach is integral to inclusive practice but Roberts-Holmes (2009) points out that despite the rhetoric of play within both the English EYFS and the Foundation Stage in Wales, they each nevertheless focus on outcomes. He highlights the barriers to genuine inclusion and participation presented by too much emphasis on early assessment and targets.

SUMMARY

Early Years settings have increasingly become the focus of broader political objectives and subject to initiatives targeting a range of social issues. Greater investment is based on the hope that early intervention can pay dividends in the long term by improving educational attainment and preventing many problems in later life. The long-term benefits of early intervention are supported by evidence from the EPPE project (Sylva et al., 2010) which demonstrates the positive outcomes for children attending high-quality settings. Measures to improve quality such as an increased focus on the workforce and a regulatory framework overseen by Ofsted inspection have been justified by this research base. The introduction of a standardised Early Years curriculum in each of the four countries of the UK is also part of the quality agenda although the variety of ways in which the curriculum may be approached demonstrates the importance of skilled graduate staff. Initiatives such as the CWDC and the IQF are part of the move to respond to this need as well as the development of Early Years Professional Status acknowledging the professional role of Early Years practitioners. Settings have also been affected by a rights-based outlook which recognises that equality is an essential aspect of quality and therefore active measures must be taken to ensure inclusive practice which welcomes all children.

Foley, P and Rixon, A (eds) (2008) *Changing children's services: working and learning together*. Bristol: The Policy Press.

This interdisciplinary book considers the 'what', 'why' and 'how' of integrated working as well as critically examining whether or not it is effective. There are chapters about working together for children as well as partnership with parents, putting policy into practice and professional development.

Hevey, D (2009) Professional work in early childhood, in Waller, T (ed) *An introduction to early childhood*. 2nd edition. London: Sage.

An interesting overview of the developments of qualifications for Early Years workers which discusses key issues and progress as well as challenges for the future.

MacNaughton, G (2003) *Shaping early childhood: learners, curriculum and contexts*. Maidenhead: Open University Press/McGraw-Hill Education.

This book focuses on how various philosophies and beliefs influence decisions in early childhood and provides many exercises to support critical reflection about the curriculum as well as working with parents.

McDowall Clark, R and Baylis, S (2010) The new professionals: leading for change, in Reed, M and Canning, N (eds) *Reflective Practice in the Early Years*. London: Sage.

This chapter examines the concept of a professional relating features of professionalism to the emerging role of EYPs.

Pugh, G and Duffy, B (2010) (eds) *Contemporary issues in the Early Years*. 5th edition. London: Sage.

This invaluable book is now in its fifth edition and includes chapters about quality, curriculum, partnership with parents, multi-agency working, inclusion and workforce issues among many other topics.

Whalley, M and the Pen Green Team (2008) *Involving parents in their children's learning*. 2nd edition. London: Paul Chapman Publishing.

The Pen Green Centre is an example of very effective collaboration with parents and there are many illustrative case studies contained in this book.

WEBSITES

www.early-education.org.uk
British Association for Early Childhood Education.

www.ioe.ac.uk.ecpe/eppeintro.htm
Website of the EPPE project.

www.peal.org.uk
The Parents and Early Learning project supports practitioners in working with parents. Many resources and good examples of practice available here.

www.cwdccouncil.org.uk
The Children's Workforce Development Council.

www.allfie.org.uk and www.csie.org.uk
The Alliance for Inclusive Education and the Centre for Studies on Inclusive Education both campaign for greater inclusion.

www.wgarcr.org.uk
Working Group against Racism in Children's Resources.

www.decet.org.uk
Diversity in Early Childhood Education and Training (DECET) acknowledges children's multiple identities and promotes diversity in the Early Years.

5   The community context

Through reading this chapter, you will:

- examine the impact of community on the child;
- consider moves to regenerate communities to combat social exclusion;
- increase your awareness of factors affecting local delivery of services to children and families;
- develop a greater understanding of how children are able to play an active part in their communities;
- recognise how concepts of public space impinge on children and childhood.

Introduction

The idea of community is a very emotive one and the term has become a political buzzword in recent years. In 2006 the then Labour Prime Minister, Tony Blair, created a new Cabinet position, the Secretary of State for Communities and Local Government, and New Labour's strong emphasis on regenerating and sustaining communities is similarly echoed by the Conservative Party. Taunton (2009) suggests that there is widespread concern that communities are disappearing. In this way, as a nostalgic imagining of a better past, the concept of community can be seen to have similarities with that of childhood (see Chapter 9 for consideration of the 'disappearance' of childhood).

In practice the term community can be understood in two ways: first as a physical neighbourhood or local environment but also carrying a more intangible meaning relating to social networks and a sense of belonging. It is in this last sense that the term community is used in political rhetoric to conjure up a supposed past when everybody knew each other and looked out for their neighbours' welfare. However, moves to improve and regenerate communities are focused primarily on socially-deprived neighbourhoods with the intention of reducing social exclusion and tackling poverty.

How are children's lives affected by the community?

Bronfenbrenner's ecological model of childhood (1979) demonstrates clearly how a child's everyday life is embedded within the community, or exosystem (see Chapter 1, page 13). This affects children in a wide range of ways from the built environment to their parents' employment. For instance, the closing down of traditional industries such as coal mining, shipbuilding and steel works in the 1980s had consequences for communities which continue to impact on children born decades later. More recently, a global recession has affected employment as many businesses such as car manufacturing are threatened with closure. Many other factors also affect a child's experience of community, such as the degree of cultural diversity they are exposed to.

ACTIVITY **1**

Take a large piece of paper and draw yourself as a child.

Fill in the details of your community and identify the impact of each of these on your life.

How many of these were you conscious of as a child and how much did you simply take for granted?

Demographics is the name given to the study of the population. Demographic data show specific characteristics of human populations such as age, sex, income and education and enable information to be gathered about different socio-economic groups. Examining data and statistics about the population in different regions can help illuminate how children's life chances are affected by the community in which they grow up. For instance, there is a greater proportion of low income families in the North East, the West Midlands and Inner London than other areas of England (Bayliss and Sly, 2009). Children born into low income families have a much higher chance of dying in their first year of life and this is twice as likely for the children of unskilled workers as for those of professionals (Freeman et al., 1999).

The impact of the local community affects not only the child's immediate health and well-being but also factors such as potential educational achievement and the likelihood of teenage pregnancy. The prevalence of childhood obesity is also strongly linked to social deprivation (Bayliss and Sly, 2009). For this reason national health strategies are usually focused at regional and community level through Primary Care Teams (PCTs) and Regional Health Boards (DoH, 2004, 2008).

ACTIVITY **2**

Check out the main demographic factors for your area from one of the websites listed on page 67.

Compare these with the demographics of a completely contrasting community in another part of the UK.

What are the differences?

What are the implications for children growing up in your area?

How do these factors affect the role of professionals working with children and families?

Community level delivery is now a key feature of children's services as a result of the Children Act (DfES, 2004b) and the Every Child Matters agenda. The Laming Report (Laming, 2003) identified the failure of relevant agencies to work together as a contributing factor in the death of Victoria Climbié. The resulting Children Act enshrined in law the expectation of effective multiprofessional work with children and their families through interagency planning and delivery. Children's Services Authorities (CSAs) have replaced LEAs to oversee all aspects of children's welfare at a local level through Children's Trusts. Children's Trusts are led by a Children's Services Director and are accountable to their local communities; effectiveness is assessed through Joint Area Reviews (JAR). In this way a multi-agency approach brings together education, welfare, social services and health to work alongside providers from the private, voluntary and independent sectors through a strategy of integrated processes and delivery. Children's Trusts are expected to undertake a joint needs assessment informed by parents and children as well as professionals and are responsible for planning and delivery of local services.

The intention behind this decentralised approach is to ensure 'joined up' services at an area level and enable local authorities to meet their own neighbourhood priorities. As an example, the West Midlands has the highest proportion of under-16-year-olds (19.5 per cent) as a percentage of the population (Bayliss and Sly, 2009) and so will clearly have quite different spending priorities to a seaside resort where the population is mainly made up of elderly and retired people. However, one of the side effects of this process is that comparisons can be drawn between different communities through publication of league tables. This may cause local dissatisfaction at perceived inequalities in treatment, frequently referred to as a 'postcode lottery'. Differences in how local authorities fund their provision are an inevitable result of devolved budgets and localised services.

Because there are certain communities where children's life chances are considerably reduced, most strategies to tackle social exclusion and reduce child poverty have been targeted within specific areas of social need. The introduction of Sure Start Local Programmes (SSLPs) towards the end of the 1990s was the main means of active intervention to improve outcomes for children and their families. Each SSLP is different because they reflect local needs and circumstances, but all share common objectives in promoting the development of supportive communities and providing a range of services for parents. As one of the prime intentions of Sure Start is to counter social exclusion by encouraging parents off benefits and into paid employment, all centres include some form of childcare. Originally targeted at the 20 per cent most disadvantaged local authority wards, the original Sure Start programme has grown and become the basis for wider provision of Children's Centres. The philosophy behind such integrated services for families can best be understood in relation to notions of human capital.

THEORY FOCUS

Concepts of 'capital'

Capital is usually thought of in terms of economic capital, i.e. the financial assets which enable people (or institutions) to buy services and resources. Clearly the economic capital available is of great significance in connection with the material circumstances of a child's life. However, there are other forms of 'capital' which also act as important 'resources' and so the possession or lack of these impact on children's life chances in addition to basic income.

---

continued

Human capital refers to the skills and knowledge that people possess in themselves. Parents can help their children to acquire human capital by supporting their learning, but this is more likely to occur if parents place a value on human capital and already possess it themselves. SureStart schemes which provide literacy and numeracy classes for parents help to develop families' human capital and thus support parents to move into paid employment – ultimately helping them to acquire economic capital.

There are many different types of knowledge and skills, some of which are more socially advantageous than others. *Cultural capital* is a term associated with Pierre Bourdieu who suggested that the ability to use and exploit knowledge came largely from a person's *habitus* – their ways of behaving and the way they view the world. This is mainly a result of socialisation and so is learned from parents and one's surroundings. In order to be successful in any *field* (or social arena), it is necessary to have the relevant and appropriate knowledge (or what Bourdieu terms *legitimate knowledge*). In this way parents who know how to 'work the system' can gain advantages for their children such as access to better schools or support for a child with a disability. A parent who lacks the *legitimate knowledge* stemming from their *habitus* is unable to successfully manoeuvre in the relevant *field* to gain the same level of support.

Social capital refers to the social connection between individuals and groups which can also serve as a 'resource'. For instance, families whose interconnectedness enables them to support each other can compensate to some degree for their lack of economic resources. Examples of other kinds of social links which can provide social capital are support groups for parents of disabled children and antenatal groups. The community is particularly important in connection with social capital as a thriving community may provide supportive networks and a level of interconnectedness which can help provide opportunities and improve outcomes for children.

Bourdieu, P and Passeron, JC (1990) *Reproduction in education, society and culture.* 2nd edition. London: Sage.

Although Children's Centres are expected to meet the needs of their local community and therefore each one will be organised differently, there is a Central Core Offer which applies to all:

- Early Years provision for children from 0–5 years providing childcare for working parents;

- family support;

- child and family health services;

- parental involvement;

- links to Jobcentre Plus;

- outreach.

Consider a Children's Centre that you are familiar with.

What services do they provide for families and children?

How do these services help to develop aspects of human, cultural and social capital?

It is too early to draw detailed conclusions about the effectiveness of such early intervention measures although evaluation of Sure Start has been integral to the programme from the beginning (NESS, 2004). In general, despite limitations in failing to reach some of the most needy families, and variable success in engaging with the needs of ethnically diverse communities, it has been welcomed as a successful model showing some improved outcomes for children (Jackson and Fawcett, 2009). However, it is evident that some parents are more likely to take advantage of services than others and the ones who are missing out are the 'hard to reach' families that such programmes are designed to support. This was recognised in the 2007 evaluation which considered variations among different centres:

> ... Parents/families with greater human capital were better able to take advantage of SSLP services than those with less human capital (i.e. teen parents, lone parents, parents in workless households).

> (NESS, 2007, p.81)

The Sure Start model of bringing children's services together into one place has also been promoted within extended schools which offer 'wrap-around' care and a base for multi-agency services and family support. The Minister for Children claimed this measure would give schools a *new role at the centre of the community* (DCSF, 2007, p.1). However, the ability of schools to realistically make a difference to a community and challenge disadvantage has been questioned (Foley, 2008b). Chiosso (2008) also claims that there is an inevitable tension between such professionally driven strategic programmes and the values and principles of community development.

Community development

The drive to strengthen community support for families through integrated services has also been accompanied by moves to improve the built environment. The Social Exclusion Unit's (SEU's) report *Bringing Britain Together: a National Strategy for Neighbourhood Renewal* (SEU, 1998) identified the need to involve communities, encourage active citizenship and empower residents. Although there are some contradictions and tensions within the assumptions underpinning this action, such as the equation of social inclusion with employment (Freeman, et al., 1999), this report marked an increasing emphasis on encouraging urban regeneration. Subsequent steps have included the creation of an Academy for Sustainable Communities, the Sustainable Communities Act (2007) and the formation of a new government department, the Department of Communities and Local Government. The ethos underpinning the Sustainable Communities Act is that local people know best what is needed within their neighbourhoods but may need help from centralised government to enable action. Therefore at a community level, approaches to local regeneration differ greatly although there are expectations that all local authorities will develop specific plans to support the economic, social and environmental well-being of their local communities.

Poverty and social exclusion

Poverty and wealth clearly have a huge impact not only on children's present well-being but also their future life chances. Between 1979 and 1997, as the gap between rich and poor increased more in the UK than any other comparable country, children and families in certain areas became significantly poorer (Freeman, et al., 1999). Under these circumstances, children's entitlement to important services cannot be taken for granted. Access is usually dependent on the ability to pay which effectively excludes poor families and their children. In fact Daniel and Ivatts suggested that *It is clear children, above all, are experiencing exclusion from full citizenship in the UK* (1998, p.74).

When first elected to government in 1997, the Labour Party used this concept of 'social exclusion' in announcing their intention to combat child poverty. Prime Minister Tony Blair set up the Social Exclusion Unit to examine the problems of neglected and alienated neighbourhoods. The concept of 'social exclusion' now guides the anti-poverty agenda and includes notions of inequality, lack of opportunity and social justice (DWP, 2003).

In 1998 Labour announced their intention to eradicate child poverty by 2020 and this aim dominated childhood policy throughout their time in office. The 2004 Child Poverty Review was followed by *Ending Child Poverty: Everybody's Business* published alongside the 2008 budget. At the same time the Child Poverty Unit was created to take a cross-government approach to driving forward strategies on a local level. In June 2008 the Child Poverty Bill was introduced into Parliament to attempt to uphold these intentions through legislation.

Government figures claim some success in removing children from poverty with numbers down from 3.4 million in 1998/9 to 2.9 million by 2006/7 (DCSF, 2009). However, other sources would challenge these figures, for instance the Joseph Rowntree Foundation (2008) suggests that after some initial success the situation has now reversed and is on the increase again with almost 4 million children currently living in poverty (cited in Roberts-Holmes, 2009). Poverty affects children in all aspects of their lives from low birth weight to bad housing, poor nutrition and a greater likelihood of an unstable family situation. Poverty is also associated with lower levels of education and it is estimated that by the age of three children from deprived backgrounds are already a full year behind their wealthier peers (Roberts-Holmes, 2009).

Responses to poverty and ideas of how to tackle it depend on political ideology. Traditionally, the political left favours approaches that redistribute wealth to those in need whereas right-wing politicians have argued that such schemes create dependency. These different ideas explain varying approaches to welfare provision explored further in Chapter 6.

Although some would argue that poverty is a natural feature of any society, Roberts-Holmes (2009) challenges this. He points out that some societies (notably Scandinavian countries) have successfully tackled child poverty by sustained and deliberate investment in public services.

For more information about child poverty see www.cpag.org.uk/

This is the website of the Child Poverty Action Group, a charity campaigning for the abolition of child poverty in the UK, and is a useful source of information, statistics and resources.

The motivation behind community regeneration is very often focused on children. For instance, launching the report of a study on urban safety, the Chief Executive of the charity Living Streets said:

> It is becoming increasingly rare to see children playing out on the streets. We have effectively designed ourselves out of our own communities through urban planning that has failed to prioritise people.

(Armstrong, cited in Learner, 2009)

Women in particular are likely to become involved in community action which can be seen to directly support the welfare of children, such as developing play facilities (Chiosso, 2008). However, despite the SEU's emphasis on active citizenship, children themselves are seldom included in the process and even when their views are sought these are not necessarily taken seriously or acted upon. Under the Sustainable Communities Act (2007) local authorities are required to consult with local people about proposals but, beyond indicating that this should include under-represented groups, there is no indication of how or who to consult. In general, neighbourhood planning has always been adult-focused and decisions are made on children's behalf by adults who make assumptions about what is appropriate for children. As a result, play spaces are most likely to be sited out of the way of adults and usually concentrate on safety for the very young with little consideration of the needs of older children. Children's participation is often at a very superficial level such as choosing the colour of swing seats. However, if, instead of simply expecting them to adapt to the built environment, children are included as partners in the process, this supports intergenerational relationships and can also avoid children becoming disaffected and alienated in the future. Kettle (2008) therefore argues that children's ability to become actively engaged in neighbourhood renewal schemes brings many benefits, to both children themselves and the community, and should not be under-estimated. Nimmo (2008) suggests that encouraging and supporting young children's links to their community is increasingly important when so much of their time is spent cut off from 'real life' within childcare settings.

> ## ACTIVITY 4
>
> *Why do you think children are not involved more in community regeneration schemes?*
>
> *What are the barriers that prevent this?*
>
> *What are the assumptions that are made about children?*
>
> *See Chapter 8, page 103, for some examples of when children have been involved as participants in a meaningful way.*
>
> *You may find Hart's ladder of participation in the same chapter a useful tool for thinking about how children are enabled or prevented from participation in their communities. Freeman et al. (1999) include another version devised by children themselves.*

Children and public space

One of the reasons children are so frequently overlooked or ignored within the community is because of the ambivalent attitude towards children in public space. Matthews claims that, despite assertions to the contrary, most attempts to involve children are *half-hearted* and largely *counterbalanced by containment strategies* (2002, p.265).

The occupation of public or social space is determined and restricted by certain rules and expectations which everybody is subject to. For instance, there are buildings one can walk straight into (most shops and public entertainment facilities such as cinemas), those which you should not enter without a specific invitation or purpose (a dentist's surgery or a stranger's house) and those which are only open to certain sections of the public such as a university, a pub or the magistrates' court. These rules apply particularly to children where even in their home there may be certain expectations about the spaces which they occupy (Freeman et al., 1999)

> ## ACTIVITY 5
>
> *Discuss the issue of public space with a small group of friends or colleagues.*
>
> *Consider different kinds of public space and the unwritten rules about who is able to access it freely.*
>
> *Compare your experiences of public space as children.*
>
> *What differences can you identify between now and the past?*
>
> *What differences are there between individuals? What might be the reasons for these?*

It is perhaps within the community that the changing experience of childhood is most visible. Whereas children were once a common sight in streets, parks and town centres, increasingly they are now only present when accompanied by an adult. Chapter 2 considered Ariès' argument that adults and children led broadly similar lives in medieval times, working and playing alongside each other. In contemporary society the reverse is true and increasingly children and adults are spatially segregated (Valentine, 1996). James et al, suggest that children are particularly noticeable in relation to their location and use the analogy of a weed as a *flower that is growing in the wrong place* to describe this phenomenon.

> *To put this more vigorously we might suggest that children either occupy designated spaces, that is, they are placed, as in nurseries or schools, or they are conspicuous by their inappropriate or precocious invasion of adult territory: the parental bedroom, Daddy's chair, the public house, or even crossing the busy road. Childhood, we might venture, is that status of personhood which is by definition often in the wrong place.*

(2001, p.37)

The occupation of social space depends on real or perceived ownership and thus is determined by politics and law. As such it can never be a neutral matter but is dependent on geographies of power (Jenks, 1995). Therefore children, who as a class lack social power, are particularly likely to be 'in the wrong place'. Their physical whereabouts are almost entirely controlled by adults so that James et al. suggest that *the central issue ... in relation to childhood space is ... that of control* (2001, p.38).

The shift of children away from public space began in the nineteenth century with the introduction of compulsory education and other moves to control and constrain children – in particular the children of the poor. Increasingly, as children are banished from public spaces, childhood and domesticity have become more and more connected so that the home can be seen as both the physical and conceptual realm of childhood.

Rasmussen (2004) suggests that the concrete, physical spaces within which the everyday life of children takes place can be considered as an *institutional triangle* made up of home, school and recreational settings. She differentiates between *places for children* (i.e. places specifically designed by adults for children, such as after-school clubs) and *children's places* which are the spaces which children themselves find important and meaningful. The more that identifiable *places for children* are created, the less tolerant and accepting of *children's places* adults become, Rasmussen argues. Although children's autonomy is increasingly curbed they still attempt to challenge adult control of space, for instance by building dens where they can avoid the adults' gaze. Opportunities for children to create their own spaces has become ever more important with the massive increase in out-of-school provision where children are located under adults' supervision and their activities regulated in collective childcare institutions (Smith and Barker, 2000).

The increasing control and surveillance of children's use of space is largely fuelled by modern anxieties about the perceived safety of the outside environment and it is this which causes parents to *restrict their children's use of space excessively* (Valentine, 2004 p.29) so that they have little independent participation in the community. This prevents children's autonomous social interaction and makes them increasingly dependent on parents to provide opportunities to meet with other children. However, children are not only barred from the physical community but there is a growing perception that children are also at risk from 'virtual' communities. Communities have always been subject to reform and change as a result of technologies – for instance the printing press made possible the formation of religious groups around different interpretations of religious texts, and TV and radio enabled communities of listeners and viewers (Taunton, 2009). Now the recent digital revolution has produced anxiety about virtual communities. Not only are computers claimed to threaten children's ability to relate to real life and inhibit their social and communication skills, but at the same time adults project their fears about childhood onto the new technologies and so are as fearful of children's safety in cyberspace as they are in actual physical space.

In comparison to many other European countries Britain is not a child-friendly place. Where children are taken for granted and welcomed as part of the community elsewhere, within the UK the drive seems to be more and more towards the privatisation of childhood so that children are kept safely incarcerated within institutions such as the family, the nursery or the school. This is not only for the perceived but doubtful benefit of children themselves, but also serves the interests of an adult-oriented society. Freeman et al. (1999) suggest that such attitudes are the result of an increasing number of adults choosing not to have children so that a smaller proportion of adults feel they have any responsibility or investment in the lives of children. The situation is not helped by the media which continues to demonise poor children in particular and present them as a threat to society. From these perspectives, children in the community are frequently seen to be 'in the wrong place'. Speaking of the Highland Play Strategy, the Chief Executive of the Groundwork Trust recently stated that children are all too often seen as an *environmental problem, to be swept off the streets like litter* (cited in Kettle, 2008, p.195). These issues demonstrate the ambivalence that is felt about childhood within contemporary society and are explored further in Chapter 9.

SUMMARY

Chapter 1 considered the way in which childhood cannot be understood without reference to the social context in which it takes place. This chapter has examined the way that the community affects a child's experiences, opportunities and life chances. Concern about struggling or deteriorating communities has led to increasing emphasis on development and regeneration with a particular emphasis on areas of social deprivation. Foremost among these initiatives is the Sure Start programme which specifically focuses on areas of need to support families and improve outcomes for children. Although there have been some criticisms of Sure Start, it is generally recognised as beneficial to the parents who access available services. Other moves to create sustainable communities focus more on the built environment. Although these are usually intended to benefit children, children themselves are rarely involved in the planning or implementation of such schemes and their views are represented by adults.

It can be seen that community is a much more restricted and contested concept for children than it is for other citizens. Children's freedom has been drastically curtailed in recent years in the name of protection to the extent that children are no longer a regular sight within many local neighbourhoods. The negative consequences of this are widespread and demonstrate both the challenge and the need for neighbourhood regeneration and sustainable communities.

Kettle, J (2008) Children's experience of community regeneration, in Jones, P, Moss, D, Tomlinson, P and Welch, S (eds) *Childhood; services and provision for children*, Harlow: Pearson Longman

This chapter discusses the impact of living in a poor neighbourhood and the extent to which children are involved in community regeneration.

Holloway, S and Valentine, G (2000) (eds) *Children's geographies: living, playing, learning*. Abingdon: Routledge.

Valentine, G (2004) *Public space and the culture of childhood*. Aldershot: Ashgate Publishing.

Both these texts cover a wide range of issues in connection with the geography of childhood.

www.statistics.gov.uk
The central source for national, regional and neighbourhood statistics.

http://www.ons.gov.uk/census/index.html
Official census website for England and Wales with links to Scotland and Northern Ireland gives access to data about the whole of the United Kingdom.

www.communities.gov.uk
This government website outlines initiatives to develop community life and is also a good source of statistics and data.

www.c4eo.org.uk/
The Centre for Excellence and Outcomes in Children and Young People's Services (C4EO) is an organisation which identifies and co-ordinates local, regional and national evidence of effective practice in delivering children's services through Children's Trusts.

www.dcsf.gov.uk/everychildmatters/earlyyears/surestart/whatsurestartdoes/
Official website of Sure Start.

www.childfriendlycities.org
UNICEF's Innocenti Research Centre provides information about child-friendly cities and communities including information on good practice and initiatives, relevant publications and updates on current research.

6 The national context: children and social policy

Through reading this chapter, you will:

- consider the place of children and families within social policy;
- examine different kinds of services and the national implications of these;
- understand how political ideology affects the ways in which public welfare is managed;
- recognise the different models of social welfare that shape approaches to service provision;
- increase your awareness of the differences in provision and approach between the four nations of the United Kingdom.

The national macrosystem is the background context within which children's lives take place.

Introduction

Since the beginning of the twenty-first century children have become increasingly prominent on the national stage and early childhood has become the focus of greater attention than at any time in the past. The sheer quantity of policy and legislation introduced during this period demonstrates growing awareness of the importance of investing in services for young children and their families. At the same time children have become a smaller percentage of the UK population and by 2007 the number of under-16s became fewer than those of state pension age for the first time (Bayliss and Sly, 2009).

Hendrick (1994) suggests that in public debate only three positions exist for children – that of victim, threat or investment. Children as victims and threats are debated in Chapter 9, but perhaps the most significant construction of childhood within a national context is the child as an investment for the country. The reducing numbers of children within the population as a whole have made this focus of even greater importance as children are viewed in the role of economic assets for the future. Therefore the position of children in regard to social policy is a critical one.

Social policy and the welfare state

Social policy is the way in which a nation or state provides for the welfare of its people. It covers a wide range of services such as education, public health, housing, transport and public safety. All of these impact on the social, physical and economic well-being of children directly or indirectly. Social policy is an intensely political field because there are strongly contested views on the best way to provide public services. In particular these arguments centre on who should be eligible for particular services, under what circumstances they apply and how welfare is to be paid for.

Fiona Williams (1989) has suggested that there are three organising principles of welfare which she identifies as family, nation and work. Children's role is clear in each of these where they are often viewed as the future of the nation or in terms of the future workforce, but primarily they are understood in their role within the family. Chapter 3 introduced the concept of familialisation of childhood (Qvortup, 1994) whereby the category of 'children' is generally subsumed into the concept of 'family'. This is particularly evident within national policy where services for children and families are treated as if they were the same thing and services for children are generally delivered through the medium of the family.

The modern welfare state, as the umbrella under which social policy is delivered was the vision of William Beveridge. In 1942, while Britain was involved in the Second World War, Beveridge wrote a report setting out a suggestion of how all working people might pay a small weekly contribution which would then enable benefits to be paid to those who were sick, unemployed and retired. The Beveridge Report's proposals were intended to prevent anyone from falling below a certain minimum standard of living and protect them from the five social evils of want, disease, squalor, ignorance and idleness. In 1945, at the end of the Second World War, a newly elected Labour Government adopted the Beveridge Report's recommendations pledging that this would enable people to be provided for 'from cradle to grave'. The launch of the National Health Service in 1948 is an example of this national commitment to provide welfare services which are free at the point of delivery.

The Beveridge Report demonstrates an approach to welfare grounded in a view of state responsibility for the well-being of the population. Such concepts are explored later in this chapter but it is interesting at this point to note the strong parallels between Beveridge's five social evils and the five outcomes of the 2004 Children Act.

The Beveridge Report	Every Child Matters
Want	Achieving economic well-being
Disease	Being healthy
Squalor	Staying safe
Ignorance	Enjoying and achieving
Idleness	Making a positive contribution

ACTIVITY 1

Consider Williams' three organising principles of social policy – family, nation and work (1989).

In what ways did the social evils identified by Beveridge undermine the interests of the family, the nation and the workforce?

How are they supported by the five outcomes of the Children Act 2004?

Each of Williams' three aspects interconnects and national investment in one area can also support another. For instance, when emergency wartime food rationing was introduced in 1940, the Prime Minister Winston Churchill suggested there could be 'no finer investment for any community than putting milk into babies'. This proposal implied that the milk was intended not only to benefit babies themselves, but would also reap dividends for the country as a whole. Such an outlook continued throughout the post-war years with the School Milk Act 1946 providing free milk for all school children under the age of 18. The supply of milk was later withdrawn from secondary schools and eventually Margaret Thatcher, in her role as Education Minister, stopped it for children over the age of seven in 1971. This is an illustration of the ongoing debate about who should benefit from services and whether they should be provided universally to everyone or only targeted at particular groups of people.

THEORY FOCUS

Universal and selective services

There are two ways in which state support may be made available to people – as either universal or selective services.

Universal services are those which are available to everyone who needs them – examples are the NHS and the education system. The intention behind this is to promote social integration and unity. For instance, this was a prime motivating factor behind the Beveridge Report which raised public morale in the war years.

Universal services are funded from taxes and National Insurance contributions. They are often associated with a specific 'trigger' – for instance pregnancy makes women eligible for a range of maternity benefits and services. Another trigger is age – children become eligible for nursery or school and older people can claim their pension, according to birth date.

As well as the benefits of social cohesion, universal benefits avoid stigma and reduce administrative costs.

Selective services are those that are targeted at the most needy – for instance social security benefits or free school meals. Although selective services are usually introduced in response to concerns that universal services are too expensive, in fact they can be costly to administer. This is because they require some form of assessment to determine who is eligible as well as 'gatekeepers' to apply means tests. Selective or targeted services can also carry a social stigma because recipients become identified as failing to cope.

ACTIVITY 2

Current health guidelines recommend that everyone should eat at least five portions of fruit or vegetables a day.

Consider the benefits and disadvantages of supplying free fruit to:

- *all children;*
- *only children from economically deprived backgrounds.*

Childcare as a social concern

ECEC has dominated the arena of childhood services since New Labour were elected to government in 1997. Their National Childcare Strategy, launched in 1998, demonstrated a commitment to expansion and improvement which continued throughout the following decade. Although it is usually presented as a service for young children, in reality childcare serves a wider political agenda relating to the economy and employment. A European network commission, set up to look at ways in which employment and family responsibilities might be reconciled, specifically stated that *good quality services are a necessary part of the economic and social infrastructure* (cited in Penn, 1999).

ECEC is a good illustration of Williams' (1989) three categories of family, nation and work. Childcare might be regarded as a service to working families or alternatively as a necessity for the workforce by freeing employees from responsibility for children during working hours. It might also be viewed as a national investment, either in the long term by supporting a more qualified future workforce, or in the shorter term through increased productivity and decreased social security benefits. This multipurpose function of childcare means that provision, funding and the position of working mothers have often been confused and contradictory.

Attitudes towards mothers who work outside the home have a great impact on the provision of childcare (Baldock et al., 2009). This was considered in Chapter 3 in relation to workplace nurseries during and in the years immediately following the Second World War. Traditionally women were used as a flexible source of labour to be taken on in part-time, casual roles when demand was high and dismissed when no longer needed. Women were expected to prioritise the care of their children, as was evident in the recommendations of the Plowden Report (CACE, 1967). Although clear about the benefits of nursery provision, the report stressed that this must only be part time so that women who had no need to work would not use it as an excuse to do so. Even in 1991, Angela Rumbold, also an advocate of quality Early Years provision, stated that it should not be regarded as a way of enabling women to work (Moss and Penn, 1996).

With no national availability of childcare what provision there was developed in a very piecemeal fashion, much of it emerging from the PVI sector. Playgroups, initially started up in the 1960s by groups of mothers in church halls and similar premises, are an example of this. The original movement grew and developed to become the Pre-School Learning Alliance (PLA) and its success has been seen by some to enable successive governments to ignore calls for nursery education (Jackson and Fawcett, 2009).

The impact of feminism has extended opportunities for women to the extent that their role has increasingly come to be seen in terms of paid employment. In fact there is evidence to suggest that the recent global recession has increased women's role in the labour market to compensate for loss of overall family income (Qureshi, 2009). In these circumstances, without a national commitment to publicly funded services, Brannen and Moss, (2003) suggest that childcare has become a commodity to be bought and sold.

When first elected to government, New Labour made the development of childcare a priority. The National Childcare Strategy, introduced in 1998, laid the groundwork by creating Early Years Development and Childcare Partnerships (EYDCPs) to co-ordinate and expand local childcare provision. This was strengthened in 2004 with the publication of the *Ten Year Strategy for Childcare* (HM Treasury, 2004) extending entitlement for 3–4 year-olds. Among other aims, the strategy planned to mainstream provision developed under Sure Start Local Programmes to create Children's Centres in every community. Alongside moves to increase provision in quantitative terms were policies to ensure quality, informed by evidence of good practice such as the EPPE project (Sylva et al., 2004). Such policy initiatives included Birth to Three Matters (DfES, 2002), later incorporated into the Early Years Foundation Stage (DfES, 2007), and a commitment to the development of the children's workforce. One of the barriers to the development of ECEC was the separation of care and education with different budgets and ministerial responsibility. Various moves attempted to overcome this artificial division such as placing Early Years settings under the regulation of Ofsted and bringing all Early Years services together in one government department – renamed the Department for Children, Schools and Families (DCSF) when Gordon Brown took over leadership from Tony Blair. Thus it can be seen that in the years following 1997, childcare moved from a peripheral concern of parents to a key place in national strategy.

ACTIVITY 3

The provision of affordable childcare has become a major factor in the drive to reduce social exclusion.

List and consider what options are available to a government to bring this about.

What would be the implications of these different options?

Think about aspects such as quality, affordability, accessibility to families, conditions for practitioners, etc.

Quality childcare is expensive and universal provision would require massive state investment. The solution in the UK has been to rely on the private sector to make up the shortfall of places and to depend on regulatory systems and legislative frameworks to maintain standards. However, this model of provision leaves parents at the mercy of the private market and raises particular difficulties for lower income households. For instance, a recent survey estimated that such families need to spend 20 per cent of their income on childcare as opposed to approximately 8 per cent for higher earners (Daycare Trust, 2008). Working Tax Credit is an attempt to tackle the issue of affordability by subsidising costs for poor families but the system is only partially successful (Pugh, 2010).

A number of commentators have criticised the tensions inherent in the increasing role of the private sector and drawn attention to the threat that this represents to quality (Ball and Vincent, 2005; Penn, 2007). Sylva and Pugh (2005) also raised concerns that prior to a general election the commitment to quality may be overtaken by an agenda that is more focused on quantity. However, Baldock et al. (2009) suggest that, regardless of which party is in power, the expansion of childcare provision is likely to continue and with it an emphasis on family support, cross-agency co-operation and inclusion.

Political ideology

The way in which services are planned, distributed and paid for is very dependent on political ideology, in other words the values that different political parties hold and their views about how society should be organised.

Although there is a wide variety of different interpretations, political viewpoints can be generalised as either predominantly 'left' or 'right' wing. While this grossly over-simplifies matters, such terminology will be adopted here for the sake of clarity. The main distinguishing features of these different perspectives are the underlying beliefs about the role of the state. Left-wing governments traditionally believe in intervention to try to bring about a more equal society. They, therefore, favour an institutional model of welfare – that is, welfare is integrated into social mechanisms and institutions as a norm. Right-wing politicians promote 'hands off' government so that individuals are responsible for their own well-being. They take a residual, or selective, approach to welfare which only supports intervention when necessary. Models of social welfare are discussed more fully in the next section but it is evident here that the way in which any government goes about organising public services, budgets, taxation and law making is dependent on their underlying ideology. Figure 2 demonstrates this relationship.

	Left wing	Right wing
Key terminology	Social democracy Socialism Interventionism	Economic liberalism Conservativism Neo-con/Neo-liberal
Key values	Equality Social justice Co-operation	Freedom Opportunity Individualism
Role of the state	Regulation of economic activity to promote social justice Tax system redistributes wealth	De-regulation of economic activity to promote wealth creation Minimum taxation
Approach to welfare	Institutional model whereby citizens have rights to universal standards of welfare to ensure a decent standard of living for all	' Safety net' principle: residual model provides minimum welfare only, intended to prevent starvation and homelessness
Relation of the state to the individual	'Hands on' government Social responsibility Support people The state provides	'Hands off' government Individual responsibilty Leave people to themselves The market provides
Recent trends*	Synthesis of social aims and market forces such as Public Finance Initiatives (PFI), public–private partnerships, 'trickle-down' economics * claimed as both left or right by their supporters, e.g. British Labour Government 1997–2010	

Figure 2 The political spectrum

Considering the political ideology of the government in power can help explain the actions of the state at different periods. For instance, the Conservative government (in power from 1979–1997) took little interest in the under-fives, viewing children as the responsibility of their parents. New Labour's focus on the importance of early childhood represented a completely different perspective. However, their approach to the economy and public services illustrates the limitations of simplistically categorising political approaches as left or right wing. In the late 1990s, in order to be elected in a changed public climate, the Labour Party repositioned itself in a far more centrist position attempting to adopt a 'third way' (Giddens, 1998). The name New Labour reflected this change of approach as did policy, which attempted to hold on to many traditional left-wing principles while adopting a more market-led attitude to the economy. In recent years the Conservative Party has similarly presented itself as 'caring conservatives' or 'compassionate Tories' to indicate a move towards the political centre ground. Since becoming leader of the Conservatives in 2005, David Cameron stressed his party's commitment to the welfare of children and families and made clear that they intend to continue the policy directions already established.

Models of social welfare

The 'third way' referred to above was an attempt to maintain the availability of welfare provision in the face of ever-increasing demands for health and social services. Medical advances and increased expectations presented difficulties in funding which the government hoped to address through a mixed economy approach – that is, through partnerships with the private sector. The expansion of the private market within childcare has already been mentioned but such an approach to public amenities is widespread; in services ranging from health to prisons, private companies become involved in the provision of state services as a profit-making enterprise. This tactic, which may be seen either as an unsatisfactory compromise or else a practical synthesis of left- and right-wing traditions depending on one's political viewpoint, demonstrates the dominance of neo-liberal ideas resulting from globalisation (see Chapter 7). Neo-liberal economic theory is the idea that individuals should be enabled to create their own wealth and that economic growth stems from healthy competition. This is a prevailing principle within many international political and economic institutions – particularly those of the UK and US. From this perspective, public services take on a business approach where clients are treated as customers and cost cutting is a prime consideration. An example of this approach is school lunches, once the remit of the local authority, which are now subject to competitive tendering.

A neo-liberal stance views wealth acquisition and employment as personal responsibilities and the result of individual endeavour. The position of the state is to provide the frameworks which will enable such enterprise to take place. Tomlinson (2008) argues that under such circumstances inequality for some children may be an inevitable outcome. Therefore it can be seen that it is not simply political viewpoints which affect the provision of public welfare, but also the ideological background within which such provision is set that shapes the model of social welfare a country adopts.

Models of social welfare

Gøsta Esping-Anderson (1989, 1986) developed a typology, (a system of categorisation based on shared characteristics), to explain the differing frameworks within which capitalist countries organise their approach to welfare. He identified three basic models.

- Social democratic model – this is where universal welfare is provided by the state. Such a model is primarily in evidence in the Nordic countries where high levels of taxation enable a correspondingly high standard of public services to be provided.

- Liberal model – this is the free-market organisation of welfare intended to keep state expenditure at a minimum. Individuals are expected to provide for themselves and their families and the state only steps in when it is essential. An example is the provision of food stamps in the USA where this form of welfare is predominant. The beneficiaries of this model are usually low-income working-class families.

- Conservative/corporatist model – this model of welfare occurs in Germany and Austria where corporations such as the Church and the family are supported by the state in providing welfare. Employers and employees pay contributions for health care and unemployment insurance and costs to service users are mainly paid for by these insurance schemes.

Hill and Tisdall (1997) point out how these models of social welfare inevitably oversimplify the situation and that elements of all three can be identified within UK provision.

Esping-Anderson's model has been criticised for oversimplifying complex social systems and ignoring gender issues. It has been developed further by Aiginger and Guger (2006) to take recent changes in the European Union into account. They argue that a new European model is emerging which combines welfare, sustainability, efficiency and economic incentives and suggest the following groupings.

- Scandinavian Model (for example, Denmark, Finland, Norway, Sweden) is the social democratic model identified above, characterised by high employment rates with the emphasis on redistribution and social benefits financed by high taxation.

- Continental Model (for example, Austria, Belgium, France, Germany) where employment is also emphasised as the basis for social transfer but with not as much emphasis on redistribution so those outside employment are less accounted for.

- Anglo-Saxon Model (for example, Ireland, United Kingdom) is an attempt to combine elements of welfare with a liberal model and emphasises the importance of individual responsibility with targeted, means-tested social benefits.

- Mediterranean Model (for example, Greece, Portugal, Spain) where responsibility for family welfare mainly rests with the family and there are limited social benefits and low employment rates for women.

- Catching-up Model (for example, Czech Republic, Hungary) refers to newly incorporated EU member states which are relatively much poorer and where new forms of welfare are only just emerging to replace the traditional socialist forms of social support.

continued

THEORY FOCUS *continued*

Esping-Anderson, G (1989) *The three worlds of welfare capitalism*. Cambridge: Polity Press.

Aiginger, K and Guger, A (2006) The European Socioeconomic model, in Giddens, A, Diamond, P, and Liddle, R, (eds) *Global Europe, social Europe*. Cambridge: Polity Press.

ACTIVITY 4

Using concepts of political ideology (Figure 2) and models of social welfare, explain why:

- *a Labour government brought in the NHS in 1948;*
- *the right to free school milk was curtailed under a Conservative ministry;*
- *under New Labour, private nursery chains experienced massive growth.*

Esping-Anderson's typology is specifically based on capitalist countries (and so, implicitly, is that of Aiginger and Guger). Changes of government affect political priorities and the ways in which services are provided and the economy is managed, but regardless of differing values, politics in the UK is shaped by the capitalist system in which it operates. Although left-wing politicians do not usually embrace capitalism with the overt enthusiasm of the right wing, it nonetheless exerts a powerful influence on the way the national economy works. This is evident in the way that a global downturn in the economy has far-reaching effects on all social structures. Cuts in public spending are inevitable as governments try to artificially shore up the banking system whose loans and borrowing underpin material consumption and economic growth. As a consequence less public money is left to invest in services.

A model of social welfare which rejects capitalism as the underpinning economic system is communism. Communist countries retain state control of resources to ensure equality of opportunity and the collective good rather than individual enterprise. Communist states have historically been viewed in negative terms by the capitalist West, but their public services may be much more advanced. Health provision in Cuba remains so good, for example, that Cuba is able to make free health care available to other South American countries. In contrast, the collapse of communism in Eastern Europe after 1989 to be replaced by a capitalist market economy led to a notable reduction in both the availability and the quality of childcare (Penn, 2005). However, capitalism as an ideology has become so deeply ingrained in contemporary Britain *that any alternative to capitalism is considered outlandish* (Ali, 2009, p.4).

Marxism and conflict theories

Marxism is a socio-economic and political system which developed from the ideas of German social theorist Karl Marx (1818–1883). Marxism (or communism) offers an alternative to the market driven, capitalist economic system. Instead, resources are held in common for the greater good of all. Communism and socialism share some similar political values but whereas socialism aims to bring these about through political action and reform, Marxism presumes social changes will happen as a result of revolution. Marx believed economic forces to be the main impetus behind social relations and that those who control the economy also control other aspects of society, such as the education system, access to health services and the media.

Marx and his life-long collaborator Friedrich Engels set out their political vision in *The Communist Manifesto* of 1848. Marx suggested that communism is historically inevitable as the final stage of society where the proletariat (i.e. workers), would rise up and seize power from the bourgeoisie – the owners of the means of production. Ruling in their stead, the proletariat would establish a free society, no longer split by artificial class divisions, in which the latent potential of everyone could be realised and social justice would prevail. Private ownership would be done away with and goods and services produced to meet people's needs rather than simply for the purpose of exchange and sale. Consequently the social causes of alienation under capitalism would be eliminated and human beings could reach fulfilment. Or – as Marx expressed it – *From each according to his abilities, to each according to his needs*.

Marx's ideas stemmed from the particular historical circumstances in which he wrote, a time of industrial-based economies. Advanced capitalism as experienced in a twenty-first century globalised economy is somewhat different and contemporary Marxist thinkers continue to adapt ideas to explain current developments. Therefore in the UK, although some remnants of political communism remain, Marxism has become primarily an academic and theoretical stance. Within Europe as a whole there is still a heritage of Marxist principles and active communist parties influence politics to a greater or lesser degree in a number of countries. However, as a political sytem, communist regimes established in the name of Marxism frequently became repressive and authoritarian in order to maintain control.

Marxism is a *conflict theory*. Conflict theories became important as explanations of social change after the decline in the popularity of functionalism (see Chapter 3, page 34). Whereas functionalists viewed society primarily in terms of unity and consensus arising from shared values and norms, Marxism emphasises the conflicts which are inevitable between different groups with opposing interests. Conflict theories critique the broad sociopolitical system, highlighting the social, political or material inequality of social groups. Feminism is another conflict theory which, like Marxism, draws attention to the ways in which dominant ideology, or traditional viewpoints, serve to make power differentials between different social groups seem natural and inevitable (see Chapter 3 for further discussion of feminism).

The impact of devolution

While children have increasingly come to the fore of the national policy focus over the last decade, traditionally there was nobody in a position of authority able to champion their interests. Over the past few years, however, the role of an advocate to speak for children and their welfare has been developed and the first UK Children's Commissioner was appointed in Wales in 2001. Northern Ireland followed suit in 2003 and then Scotland in 2004. In 2005 a Children's Commissioner was appointed for England, although the Commissioner has a weaker role than in other countries, including the rest of the UK (Handley, 2009).

Although in discussing national policy towards children this chapter has mainly referred to the UK as if it represents a unified approach, this is a misleading assumption to make (Clark and Waller, 2007). The example of Children's Commissioners demonstrates how there are considerable differences between the separate countries of the UK and the Republic of Ireland resulting in increasingly varied policies in respect of young children and families. The Republic of Ireland has been an independent country since 1922 with its own constitution, government and currency (the euro). Consequently the Republic has quite different structures, curriculum and training to the rest of the British Isles. However, the UK (made up of the countries of England, Wales, Scotland and Northern Ireland) was ruled centrally from London. Past governments were generally opposed to devolution – that is, the passing of decision-making from central to regional authorities. This attitude changed under New Labour and the Northern Ireland Assembly was established in 1998 to govern Northern Ireland, closely followed by the creation of the Scottish Executive and the National Assembly of Wales, both in 1999. However, because the majority of the UK population live in England, English policy is often mistakenly referred to as if it applied everywhere.

Devolution and an increased focus on the Early Years have developed in parallel and so devolved government offered new opportunities for policy development as each country was starting from a low baseline of provision. In the main, concerns have been similar so that, for instance, although the Child Poverty Bill is intended to be UK wide it is recognised that Wales and Scotland already have ambitious anti-poverty agendas of their own. Similarly Northern Ireland, Wales and Scotland all have their own equivalents of Ofsted to oversee standards although each of these works in a slightly different way. Baldock et al. (2009) point out how, although not invariably the case, devolved authorities have frequently been ahead of England in introducing new initiatives.

Developments throughout the UK and the Republic of Ireland have not happened in isolation and increased international recognition of the importance of Early Years provision has affected developments in each country. Each nation influences and is influenced by the rest of the UK. For instance, the Welsh Assembly government pioneered new approaches to safeguarding children which influenced the 2004 Children Act but the Welsh Code of Practice for children with special needs derives from the English one.

Wales places a particularly strong emphasis on the importance of play and has led the way in play since 2002 when the National Assembly of Wales made it the first country in the world to produce a policy specifically related to play. The definitions of play work set out in this document have informed professional practice ever since.

While Wales has championed play, the emphasis in Scotland, where there is a designated Minister for Children and Early Years, has been on integration and the Scots pioneered integrated approaches long before there were such expectations in England (Baldock et al., 2009). The Scottish focus on continuity is also evident in the development of a curriculum from 3–18 to replace 5–14 guidelines. Northern Ireland, too, places an emphasis on continuity and progression for children through the Early Years and school system and has also developed a number of joint initiatives with the Republic of Ireland, in particular in the area of special needs.

The different emphases of devolved authorities have usefully contributed to the ongoing debate about early childhood services. This has enabled different governments to develop particular strengths and also given them the opportunity to focus on regional issues and priorities. An example is the fact that whereas children in Wales had the worst well-being in the UK in 2005, poverty rates have fallen faster than in England and Scotland and now reflect those of the rest of the UK (Wyn Siencen and Thomas, 2007).

Reed (2009) points out that although there are considerable differences among the four nations of the UK, it is important to also note the significant similarities and shared values as they draw towards a common consensus on the services which children should receive.

ACTIVITY 5

Consider the issues raised by devolution.

What are the benefits? What are the challenges?

SUMMARY

Services and policy for children are frequently conceived of in terms of national investment for the future and although children are now a central feature of national policy, they are often not accounted for as individuals but regarded as part of a family unit (Daniel and Ivatts, 1998). As a result, services which purport to benefit children, such as Early Years provision, are actually designed to meet a number of competing agendas.

The ways in which public services are organised and provided are dependent on the values and beliefs of those in a position of power. Therefore political ideology shapes provision in terms of who is entitled to receive services as well as how these should be paid for. Social welfare in the UK attempts to straddle the middle ground between a liberal philosophy which expects people to take responsibility for their own well-being and universal services which support social equity.

Since the beginning of the twenty-first century the individual countries which make up the UK and Republic of Ireland have increasingly begun to develop varying approaches towards children's services which reflect regional concerns and priorities. The shared value base which underpins this means that there is much to learn from each other's good practice.

Baldock, P, Fitzgerald, D and Kay, J. (2009) *Understanding Early Years policy*. 2nd edition. London: Sage.

A very readable book which explains how policy is made and translated into practice. Highly recommended.

Brannen, J and Moss, P (eds) (2003) *Rethinking children's care*. Buckingham: Open University Press.

A complete overview of the political and theoretical issues in regard to the provision of childcare including many useful examples.

Clark, MM and Waller, T (2007) *Early childhood education and care: policy and practice*. London: Sage.

A very useful examination of the policy situation in the four countries that make up the UK.

Hendrick, H (ed) (2005) *Child welfare and social policy*. Bristol: The Policy Press.

A good outline of the concepts, issues, policies and practices that affect child welfare.

Pugh, G (2010) The policy agenda for early childhood services, in Pugh, G and Duffy, B (eds) *Contemporary issues in the Early Years*. 5th edition. London: Sage.

This chapter provides a summary of the main developments in national policy in recent years, explaining how current provision and legislation has come about and identifying challenges for the future.

www.ncb.org.uk
www.daycaretrust.org.uk
Both of these charities undertake research and influence policy and are good sources of information on public policy regarding children and families.

www.theyworkforyou.com
A website that covers political issues where you can find official statements and transcripts of debates as well as details such as the voting record of your local MP.

www.childreninwales.org.uk
www.childreninscotland.org.uk
www.ci-ni.org
These websites give more information about the devolved nations of the UK.

7   The global context

Through reading this chapter, you will:

- consider how international comparisons help us examine the assumptions underlying practice and to learn from others;
- recognise the dangers of making universal assumptions about childhood which cannot be applied globally;
- develop greater awareness of global inequalities and the ways in which children can be disproportionately affected by the impact of globalisation;
- understand the extent to which versions of childhood are dependent on economic circumstances.

Introduction

This chapter will consider childhood from a global perspective. The improvement in children's lives over the past century in line with increasing economic prosperity can blind us to the fact that the situation of the majority of the world's children is very different. Those who study childhood or who work with children have access to a huge body of knowledge and expertise, but it is important to remember that what we 'know' about children is based on norms of child development and child-rearing patterns in affluent industrialised countries. Very different constructions of childhood exist across the world and it is dangerous to make global assumptions based on our own limited and highly selective perspective.

The benefits of international comparisons

International perspectives enable us to compare a variety of systems and critically analyse current policy and practice and the implications of this for children (Waller, 2009). For instance, Hohmann's account of recent developments in the German Early Years workforce (2010) helps us to think about similar policy initiatives which are happening in the UK. In contrast, a very different picture emerges from Burr (2004) in her report of how children's rights are interpreted and applied internationally, particularly among children in Vietnam. Burr argues that imposing westernised ideas of protected childhoods can actually work to undermine children's independence and well-being. This example demonstrates another benefit of international comparisons – they also make us question our own assumptions, so that we can be clearer about our values and principles rather than making judgements based on taken-for-granted customs.

It is, however, important when approaching any international comparisons to bear in mind the ways in which understandings of childhood are shaped by cultural beliefs (see Chapter 1). Pound et al. (2009), reviewing how learning is organised in diverse countries across the globe, draw attention to the way in which this is affected by cultural–historical perspectives. They argue that research and knowledge is usually framed in ways which favour European social practices without acknowledging how culturally specific this is. Similarly, Rogoff (2003) points out how cultural features are often treated as if they were quite separate from underlying principles. She warns that data cannot be interpreted without taking cultural assumptions into account. For instance, child observations always take place within a *context* and this context is made up of particular beliefs about childhood. As a result, certain aspects will be focused on and others ignored or not even noticed depending on values and priorities. As an example, UK provision focuses far more on literacy and numeracy than do Scandinavian practitioners who also resist the assessment of children so integral to British practice. This is because Nordic countries regard childhood as important in its own right, whereas in the UK Early Years provision is often viewed as a foundation for the child's *future* success.

Provided you remain aware of your own specific cultural 'lens', it is very useful to examine and think critically about practice from other countries. There have been a number of reports and reviews of international provision (see suggestions for further reading on page 92) which enable comparisons to be made and particular aspects evaluated. These can be very revealing in terms of cultural values and ideas about childhood. For instance, Bennett (2003) identifies two different curricular approaches to the Early Years which he calls 'social pedagogy' and the 'infant school approach'. The first of these is active and experiential, focusing on the whole child and emphasising the outdoor environment, whereas the second concentrates on adult-led play activities to achieve specific aims and prepare for school. The social pedagogy approach is used in Scandinavian countries whereas the UK and USA (as well as a number of European countries such as France, Belgium and Holland) focus on the second. The benefit of learning from other countries' practice can be seen in the way in which aspects of the social pedagogical approach have been integrated into the Early Years Foundation Stage (DfES, 2007) as well as in developing the role of EYPs. A greater emphasis on the outdoor classroom and increasing value given to outdoor play has also come about as a result of studying Scandinavian approaches such as Forest schools. The influence of the Reggio Emilia approach (Abbott and Nutbown, 2001) also demonstrates how the UK has responded to international practice.

ACTIVITY *1*

Log on to the website of the Organisation for Economic Co-operation and Development (OECD, see page 92 for web addresses) and look at the Thematic Review of Early Childhood Education and Care Policy.

Compare different aspects of provision across the countries which are included in this review, such as curriculum, age groups, staff qualifications and funding.

Can you form any conclusions about different countries' priorities and views of the child?

Are you able to apply any of the ideas considered in relation to models of social welfare (Chapter 6) to these findings?

Globalisation and childhood

Globalisation now enables much greater co-operation and sharing of perspectives and research across the world. But this also poses a danger as provision and practice in some regions may be judged unfavourably in relation to that prevalent in prosperous areas. Many countries are not in a position to provide the same form of childhood and Boyden draws attention to the issue of setting *global standards and ... common policies* (1997, p.214) which are based on the priorities and concerns of more powerful nations.

THEORY FOCUS

What is globalisation?

Globalisation is the term used to describe how modern economic systems and technology enable trade and the financial markets to operate on a global scale. In this way, finance and commerce operate as if the world makes up a single economic system. This market is dominated by huge multinational corporations who have the power to switch their operations to wherever labour and materials are cheapest in order to increase profits. As a result, they wield an extraordinary amount of power. The USA, as the world's wealthiest country, is the headquarters of the majority of multinationals and many brands such as Coca Cola and McDonald's are promoted all over the world. Many criticisms of globalisation relate to the way in which this amounts to 'cultural imperialism' as American commodities and values gradually displace local goods and traditions. Those who argue that globalisation is harmful point to the ways in which globalised markets increase poverty in the poorest counties by controlling resources and increasing the gap between rich and poor; whereas those in favour see it as the way in which poor countries can benefit from international trade and develop economically.

Penn (2004) argues that globalisation disproportionately affects children because they are particularly vulnerable to the effects of poverty. She points out how the customary micro-level approach of practitioners assumes that socio-economic change is the role of politicians and economists and unrelated to their own practice. However, these wider factors are often more influential in terms of children's life chances than local practice may be.

It is important to remember that while the main focus of research is on relatively rich Western societies (which are also the source of most of the theories and concepts of children's needs and development), 80 per cent of the world's children live in very different circumstances (Penn, 2005). This raises questions about society's expectations of children and the diverse models of childhood that exist across the world. As James and James (2008) point out, the Western childhood is a minority experience. For this reason they recommend using the term *the majority South* when referring to poorer areas of the world. This is also the terminology preferred by NGOs (non-governmental organisations, such as Oxfam for instance) and other agencies working in these regions. However, despite being quite foreign to the lives of the mass of children, the privileged minority model promotes an ideology of 'proper' childhood:

This model of childhood constructs healthy childhood as one that orientates the child towards independence rather than interdependence, towards school-based learning rather than work-based learning, and separates them from the wider forces of politics, economy and society.

(Wells, 2009, p.4)

The predominance of this perspective results in other models of childhood not being recognised as valid. This has the effect of *penalising, or even criminalising* the childhoods of the poor (Boyden, 1997, p.207).

ACTIVITY 2

Travelling in India I once attempted to buy fruit in a market from an elderly lady who had evidently limited experience of Europeans. Appearing very anxious, she called for her grandson who was about five years old. He confidently added up my bananas and oranges and told me, in English, that it came to 'seven and ten rupees'. I smiled and said 'Oh, seventeen' and he repeated the word 'seventeen' with a grin. When I handed over a couple of notes he looked at them carefully then counted out my change, thanked me and ran off to continue the game he had been playing.

Consider all the things the boy was learning through this brief interchange.

Compare it with the situation of a British five-year-old who 'actively' learns about money through role play in their classroom.

What are the different assumptions about childhood that are apparent in each case?

Western views of the majority South tend to take a protectionist stance which assumes that working childhoods are automatically wrong by definition and should be replaced with the model of childhood prevalent in developed nations. Although well-meaning in intent, this view can be seen as condescending and even arrogant. It shows limited understanding of the realities of many people's lives and circumstances, as well as an ethnocentric assumption that what is familiar to us is necessarily the best for others. One outcome of such viewpoints is that you may sometimes hear people say that children in poorer regions of the world 'do not have a childhood' or they may even use such emotive phrases as 'lost' or 'stolen' childhoods. While it must be recognised that a great many children do suffer greatly, as will be considered later in this chapter, the use of such emotional rhetoric is patronising and unhelpful.

Most of the images of childhood from the majority South which are available in other parts of the world are from news reports or charity appeals. There are very few images of happy, healthy children going about their daily lives, such as the boy in the market mentioned above. This serves to reinforce ideas of poverty and devastation as the norm across much of the world. As a result, the images we are most familiar with are stereotypes of suffering children: Wells (2009) identifies this 'spectacle' as 'the politics of pity'. News footage and pictures in the newspapers emphasise catastrophes and upheavals where children are included for symbolic value to illustrate the horrors being reported. On the other hand, photographs for charity campaigns frequently depict two distinct types of image: both the suffering child, in need of food, water, shelter or medicine and smiling groups of children 'afterwards'. These are designed to elicit donations by appealing to the viewer's conscience and to give donors a warm feeling of having made a difference. In this way, large-scale campaigns such as Red Nose Day and Comic Relief can serve to perpetuate the social construction of 'the third world child'. Wells (2009) suggests that there are many parallels between such campaigns and the child- saving movements of the nineteenth century (see Chapter 2, p.25).

ACTIVITY **3**

Make a collection of images and stories of children from the majority world.

How much of the imagery conveyed is positive?

How many emphasise poverty, illness and disease, war and disasters?

Look in particular at pictures of babies.

How do they compare to photographs of Euro-American babies in the media, for instance in advertising and magazine features?

What is the effect of this difference?

Consider the sources of the material you have gathered.
To what extent does this affect the nature of the implied message?

How children are affected by global inequalities

Penn (2005) draws attention to the way in which Western views of childhood are based on an expectation that adults will protect children and create a secure environment for them. However, as she points out, *most of the world's children grow up in environments that are far from benign* (2005 p.99). Although in the UK and Europe, children form a dwindling proportion of the population, elsewhere in the world they are in the majority and globally we have the largest child population in history (Gabriel, 2007). This makes the position of children within less developed countries very different to that taken for granted in the minority world; indeed many children have responsibilities for themselves and family members which are quite unknown to the cosseted children of more prosperous societies.

Poverty is the overriding cause of most of the problems facing children in the majority South; but poverty is not simply a matter of lack of money as it may appear in more consumer-oriented societies. In societies which lack effective systems and services and where employment may be unpredictable, families are entirely dependent on each other for welfare and survival. In such circumstances poverty can be life-threatening; for instance, without access to health resources, infant, child and maternal mortality rates are high and it is estimated that about 10.5 million children die each year before their fifth birthday (UNICEF, 2006). Many of the diseases which threaten children could be prevented but few parents can afford to buy medicines. As a result, drug companies in the West are often reluctant to invest in developing drugs to combat malaria and other diseases which claim millions of children's lives every year. HIV and AIDS have increased the plight of poor children, particularly in sub-Saharan Africa. The *British Medical Journal* points out that of the 13 million children who have been orphaned as a result of AIDS, 95 per cent of them live in Africa (cited by Penn, 2005). Drugs do exist which are effective against HIV but as prices are regulated by large multinational drug companies, these are usually only available in relatively wealthy countries. The long-term effects of such a situation for an entire generation of children left without parents are disturbing.

Apart from the direct consequences of lack of access to the resources necessary for survival, the greatest global threat to children's lives is war. Children are particularly vulnerable to conflicts and figure disproportionately highly as refugees across the world. Kaldor (1999) argues that as a result of globalisation, wars have changed form. Instead of soldiers killing each other in disputes over territory, 'new' wars are now fought to gain control of resources, such as oil or mineral wealth. She claims that the majority of those killed in 'new wars' are now civilians including huge numbers of women and children. UNICEF's statistics bear this out with figures for just one year estimated at 2 million children 'slaughtered' as well as another 6 million injured and 12 million left homeless (UNICEF, 2002).

The issue of working children

Global financial systems have led to greater inequalities of wealth, both within countries and across the world, as the economic activity of large multinational companies has come to dominate world markets. This has a particular impact on the world's poorest people whose incomes in real terms have continued to fall every year since the 1980s (UNICEF, 2002). Families struggling to find food and shelter have no money to spare for education and although parents may have aspirations for their children, their immediate priority will be the day-to-day survival of the family. In these circumstances, it is not surprising that in large areas of the world it is taken for granted that children should work and contribute to the family income.

The issue of working children is a complex and multidimensional one (Boyden et al., 1998). Many children are involved in working alongside parents in family businesses or on the land so figures are hard to calculate. The campaign group Fair Play for Children give estimated numbers of 218 million children between the ages of five and 17 years old working worldwide (www.fairplayforchildren.org).

The question of whether or not children should be economically active is frequently framed in very emotive terms; this is especially the case when it is designated 'child labour'. For instance, the website mentioned above talks in terms of children being 'rescued' from work. There is frequently an assumption that when children are working they are not at school and if they attend school then they do not work (Wells, 2009). However, this is very simplistic and does not reflect the true situation where very many will do both. Working is not necessarily bad in itself, as was evident in Activity 2 on page 84, and we need to recognise that not all child labour is exploitative. In fact many working children feel strongly that they should have a right to participate in the real world (Burr, 2004). Ironically, an increasing emphasis on education and compulsory school attendance can result in increased numbers of children working in order to afford their schooling (Boyden, 1994).

There is a big difference between children working in slave conditions in sweat shops and those who contribute to family income, as was expected within the UK in the not so distant past, so it is important not to cloud the issues with sentiment. The International Labour Organisation (ILO) recognises that children may be involved in a range of work and attempts to define certain types of economic activity as 'child work' (ILO, 2006). It must be recognised that there are many circumstances in which children certainly are exploited and the drive for high profits and cheap goods in the West is undoubtedly implicated to some extent in this. However, the situation is complex and needs to be seen in context. As Viruru (2008) points out, work is not always the worst thing that happens in children's lives and it is important to ensure that children's lives are not made worse as a consequence of stopping work. An example of this was the 'successful' consumer campaign to boycott a well-known brand of trainers because children were involved in their manufacture. As a consequence the company stopped using child labour with the result that many children turned instead to considerably more harmful employment such as child prostitution. Rather than emotional responses, it is more useful to look for realistic solutions and viable options such as ways in which work and schooling may be combined.

International action to improve the well-being of children

As most of the problems affecting childhood in impoverished countries are a direct result of poverty, strategies to alleviate suffering and improve the situation of children are primarily focused on financial solutions. The World Bank (set up to support the rebuilding of countries and economies following the Second World War) lends money to poorer countries through the International Monetary Fund (IMF) to enable them to develop their economies. However, rates of interest are very high, resulting in a heavy burden of debt. Those in favour of globalisation see economic development on a world scale as the only means by which poorer countries can become prosperous and overcome the difficulties that beset them; others believe that globalisation is primarily of benefit to large global organisations because it enables access to cheap labour and brings more consumers into the market place. Certainly the involvement of the World Bank and IMF are recognised as instrumental in the increasing poverty of much of the majority South where debt repayments make up the greatest part of many countries' budgets (Prout, 2005). They are also criticised for imposing specific conditions in Africa, Asia and South America based on the interests of powerful countries and reflecting their values.

As part of international development there has been a huge increase in programmes to improve the lives of young children by international aid agencies, charities and NGOs. Woodhead (2009) argues that early childhood care and education is now a *global phenomenon* although he recognises that discourses of the modern child sit alongside more traditional expectations for young children as contributors to their household.

Again, this shows the need to recognise the sociocultural context of children's lives because most interventions are based on westernised ideas of childhood and try to impose values that may be at odds with those of local ways of life (Burr, 2004). In this respect parallels could be drawn with targeted intervention strategies within the UK such as Sure Start, which have attracted similar critiques in terms of imposing different cultural values and a 'superior' way of life (see Chapter 5).

Nonetheless, it is evident that across the world millions of children are growing up in appalling conditions and this creates a moral imperative for action. The framework for much of this comes under the umbrella of the United Nations Convention on the Rights of the Child (UNCRC).

THEORY FOCUS

United Nations Convention on the Rights of the Child

The UNCRC was formally adopted by the United Nations in November 1989 and is the most widely endorsed treaty ever. It was ratified by the UK government in 1991 and virtually every country in the world has signed up to it, committing themselves to implement the recommendations within their laws and policies. The only exceptions are the USA and Somalia (which has no government in place to ratify a treaty).

The convention is based on 54 separate articles which outline a wide range of expectations from the right to a name and identity to protection from injury and abuse, and includes the rights of children with disabilities to enjoy a full and decent life. These rights are usually referred to as the 3 'Ps' – namely provision, protection and participation.

Franklin (2002) distinguished between welfare rights, which are mainly concerned with the child's well-being and protection, and liberty rights, which underline the child's right to make their own decisions. He states that although there is rarely any disagreement about children's welfare rights, their claims to liberty rights are frequently contested. (See Chapter 8 for further discussion of the tensions between these two sets of rights).

The UNCRC stems from a number of earlier international moves to protect children as a class. In 1914 Eglantine Jebb, the founder of Save the Children, promoted an International Charter of Children's Rights to recognise children's needs and protection from harm. Ten years later, the League of Nations set out principles for the treatment of children in the first international agreement, the Declaration of Geneva (1924), which emphasised the duties of adults towards children. Other UN moves followed such as that in 1959 when the concept of 'best interests' was introduced to protect children from exploitation. What made the UNCRC a landmark agreement was the extension of provision and protection rights to include the right to participation. In doing so the *convention contributes to the changing status of children worldwide* (Cohen, 2006; cited in Wells, 2009, p.19)

The full text of the UNCRC can be accessed online at:
www.unicef.org.uk/publications/pub_detail.asp?pub_id133

Although the intention of the UNCRC can be considered as *a benign attempt to bring enlightenment and humane standards to all children* (Prout, 2005, p.31), it is evident that it is very much rooted in Western tradition. In this way it might be seen to promote a model of a globalised ideal childhood (Boyden, 1997). James and James (2004) suggest that the UNCRC is particularly problematic in its attempt to regulate childhood across time and space, ignoring the diversity of culture. Such concerns are echoed by Wells who argues that international aid agencies are instrumental in promoting this ideal of childhood as increasingly the UNCRC is incorporated into national laws. This establishes new definitions of childhood and a *presumption that childhood can be governed at a global level* (Wells, 2009, p3).

Conflicts and tensions can arise when Western values diverge from models of childhood existing elsewhere and the implementation of children's rights needs to be considered in relation to the social and cultural context of their lives. For instance, welfare rights are based very much on a romanticised view of a childhood without responsibility. This discourse constructs the child as innocent, vulnerable and in need of adult protection. Such a model of childhood is at odds with the reality of children's lives in many parts of the world and so expectations will be very different. An example of this is the right to 'compulsory and free education'. This means that a child can be compelled to go to school – a situation taken for granted in the UK where education is recognised as the occupation of childhood and school is seen as the natural domain of children. What is considered the norm in countries with a well-developed infrastructure to support universal schooling can be more problematic in other parts of the world. In regions where schools have few qualified teachers and no resources, teaching is often reliant on rote learning and may be of limited value. As Wells (2009) points out, education is frequently viewed as the solution to a multitude of problems and an urgent priority for development. However, in reality, access to a good quality education in poorer countries, no less than developed ones, is predominantly an issue of class and social position. In such circumstances the decision to drop out of school in order to work may be a sensible and pragmatic one. In this way welfare rights can conflict with the child's right to autonomy and self-determination. (See the next chapter for further development of this debate.)

There is also a tension between the modern Western view of human rights based on the individual and Southern ideas of interdependence and communal responsibility (Burr, 2004). Whereas individualism is fundamental to British and American traditions which emphasise the individual, unique child, many cultures think instead in terms of kinship and family. Children are valued collectively as part of the family unit making it hard to reconcile children's rights as envisaged in the UNCRC with circumstances where it is the greater good of all which takes priority (Alston, 1994).

All of this can create what Burr claims is a *confused and contradictory approach* (2004, p.15) whereby many international programmes working with poor children are torn between a protectionist approach and an ethos based on children's rights. As long as such contradictions persist then families are likely to continue to follow traditional practices rather than take on new, international expectations.

ACTIVITY 4

Below is a selection of rights under the UNCRC. Discuss them with your peers and consider whether it is realistic or appropriate to attempt to create a global model for childhood.

Which rights do you think are fundamental?
Are there any that you think are problematic?

Provision:

- *care necessary for the child's well-being;*

- *the highest attainable standards of health and necessary health treatment;*

- *education that is preparation for responsible life in a free society;*

- *rest and leisure.*

Protection:

- *from injury or abuse;*

- *from unlawful deprivation of liberty;*

- *from discrimination.*

Participation:

- *contact with parents and family;*

- *freedom of expression and information;*

- *freedom of association and free assembly.*

Download a copy of the UNCRC for yourself and consider to what extent you feel children's rights are taken seriously.

The difficulties of reconciling cultural views of childhood with an internationally prescribed model suggests that in practice the UNCRC is not as universally applicable as it was intended to be. This is borne out by the fact that many countries, while signing up to the convention in principle, have not agreed with all of its provision and have entered reservations. What this means in practice is that they reserve the right to opt out of certain aspects which they believe do not reflect their own countries' values or interests. For instance, the African Congress has put in place an African Charter of Rights alongside the UNCRC to more accurately respond to the needs of African children. The UK entered reservations in connection with immigration and was also not prepared to agree to extend protection to under-18s in armed conflict. Nonetheless, the UNCRC represents a significant landmark for children as a class whereby their interests and well-being are acknowledged across the world.

Childhood is a luxury

It is important to avoid sweeping generalisations and to assume that *all* children in certain areas of the world lead lives which are adversely affected by poverty. Extremes of wealth and poverty exist everywhere – the USA for instance, although the wealthiest country in the world, has very high levels of child poverty. It is the economic circumstances which surround them that primarily determine a child's life chances and these are *more likely* to be favourable in certain areas of the world. A better approach is to recognise that what is viewed in the West as a 'good childhood' is actually a product of these socio-economic circumstances. As Goldstein (1998, p.389) points out in a comparative study of childhood in Brazil, *childhood is a privilege of the rich*. While large numbers of Brazilian children fend for themselves on the streets, those from wealthy and privileged backgrounds are cared for by poor women who must leave their own children in order to earn a living. This is a pattern of childcare that is repeated all over the world (Penn, 2004) and many poor mothers can only support their own children by travelling abroad to work as nannies and mothers' helps in rich countries in order to send money home. In these ways childhood at a global level can be seen to mirror historical developments where 'modern' childhood was something that wealthy families could afford to provide for their offspring long before such lifestyles became the norm for children of the poor (see Chapter 2).

There are many other ways in which poor countries are exploited by more powerful ones for their own gain. World trade which provides cheap food and clothing for the developed world is dependent on the availability of plentiful low-cost labour and so concentrates production in regions where many have limited power or control over their lives. Even the growth of transnational adoptions in recent years demonstrates how children from needy societies can serve as a resource for richer nations. Socio-economic systems generally favour the rich over the poor and this is just as true at a global level. Such deep inequalities raise profound ethical considerations which affect us all.

SUMMARY

The ideas about children and 'knowledge' of childhood that dominate both theory and practice are derived from a primarily Western perspective. It is essential to remember that this represents only a small percentage of the world's children. While much can be gained by a study of international comparisons, it is important to approach everything with awareness of how one's own cultural background affects the ways that information and ideas are interpreted.

The majority of the world's children live in circumstances far removed from the comfortable and protected lifestyles made possible for Western children as a by-product of affluence. Disease, lack of access to health resources and the devastation of war create problems which cannot simply be solved by the provision of educational opportunities. The UNCRC was introduced to try to ensure children's rights to provision, protection and participation are met; however, this is founded on Western values and can often conflict with local traditions and views of childhood.

FURTHER READING

Penn, H (2004) *Unequal childhood: young children's lives in poor countries.* Abingdon: Routledge.

An account of how global economic conditions affect the lives of young children in the poorest countries. Penn shows how, far from being at a distant remove, the circumstances that bring about such inequalities are directly related to our own lives. The book includes very useful chapters on poverty and issues of international aid.

Waller, T (2009) International perspectives, in Waller, T (ed) *An introduction to early childhood: a multidisciplinary approach.* 2nd edition. London: Sage.

This chapter develops an overview of reports on international comparisons of Early Years provision, identifying their key findings. Waller includes helpful charts that distinguish key differences between various countries' approach to ECEC as well as helpful summaries of Te Whāriki and the Reggio Emilia approach.

Wells, K (2009) *Childhood in a global perspective.* Cambridge: Polity Press.

Most writing about childhood is based on a Western perspective but in this book Karen Wells draws on research about children's lives across the world to show how globalisation is radically reshaping children's lives. The book contains a thought-provoking chapter on working children.

WEBSITES

www.unicef.org.uk
Website of the United Nations Children's Fund (UNICEF) which is very informative about children across the world. UNICEF publishes regular reports on 'The State of the World's Children' which are available here as is also the full text of the UNCRC.

www.oecd.org/edu/earlychildhood
The Organisation for Economic Co-operation and Development is an excellent source of comparable statistics and economic and social data.

8   The child's own context

Through reading this chapter, you will:

- understand the concept of 'child standpoint' and how children are constructed as 'other';
- consider how children might be thought of as active social actors and social agents in their own right;
- recognise some of the difficulties and conflicts that arise in connection with the competency of the child;
- consider practical ways in which practitioners can collaborate with children to support meaningful participation.

Bronfenbrenner (1979) emphasised the fact that individuals can affect the exosystem and macrosystem but in practice it is usually only adults who are considered sufficiently competent to do so. This chapter considers the agency of the child.

In 1900 Ellen Kay, a Swedish feminist, proclaimed that the twentieth century would be the *century of the child* (cited in Cunningham, 1995, p.163). Perhaps in retrospect this was rather an optimistic prediction for the time, but nevertheless by the end of the last century it would be fair to claim that childhood had become recognised as an important stage of life in its own right. Children have moved from being viewed as passive objects of study to active subjects in their own lives; their rights to participation and to have their wishes taken into account are recognised within legal frameworks at national level through the Children Acts 1989 and 2004 and internationally in the UNCRC (1989). This represents considerable change for the better, but the situation is not a straightforward story of continual improvement and progress; children's voices do not carry as much weight as those of adults and their rights to participation within society are still frequently overruled in the name of protection (Handley, 2009).

Childhood standpoint and the child as 'other'

This chapter will take a childhood standpoint perspective (Mayall, 2002); this is a viewpoint which recognises the perspective of the child as a frequently overlooked but valid and important position. The idea of 'standpoint' comes from feminism. Feminist standpoint theory rose to prominence in the 1970s and 1980s when feminist scholars drew attention to the ways in which knowledge and explanations of the world always assumed a perspective in which male experience was the norm. In this way women were constructed as 'other' (De Beauvoir, 1973) and as exceptions to the usual pattern of events. 'Othering' women resulted in their specific viewpoints and needs being ignored

– for instance, sociological theories about work which did not take into account the particular difficulties and circumstances of working mothers and ignored the great extent of women's 'hidden' work within the home. In a similar way, children's own points of view were simply not recognised for many years and their role as minors justified adults making decisions on their behalf. Chapter 3 suggested that the best interests of the child are not always necessarily the same thing as the best interests of the family; however, it was not until the 1989 Children Act that children had the right to have their perspective taken into account when decisions are made about their lives – for instance, in connection with which parent they will live after a family break up. Traditionally children's voices have been ignored and childhood and children's lives have solely been explored through the views and understandings of their adult caretakers (Christenson and James, 2008).

Although women are now (usually) considered on an equal footing with men within society, this is certainly not the case with children. If you were asked to envisage a person, you might think of a male or female, young or old and of varying ethnic origin. Everybody is likely to imagine a quite different person – but the one characteristic they will all have in common is that they will be grown up. The term 'person' assumes an adult and children are something else; they are 'other'. The concept of 'other' has been of fundamental importance in postmodern interpretations of society and has been used to examine ways in which knowledge is constructed by those with the power to have their 'truths' recognised as the dominant reality (Foucault, 1977). In this way, social institutions and structures mainly privilege white, male, able-bodied adults and consequently women, children, people from different ethnic groups and those who are disabled are viewed as 'other'.

The adult/child distinction which constructs adulthood as the norm is a useful concept to bear in mind when considering children's standpoint. Children are frequently denied a voice because their point of view is not considered as valid as that of an adult. Much of this is to do with issues of competence, which will be discussed later in this chapter, but there is also a sense in which children are not taken seriously because they are not viewed as citizens in their own right. Nick Lee goes so far as to suggest that children have traditionally not been viewed as human *beings* at all, but rather as 'human *becomings*' (Lee, 2001a, my emphasis) – in other words, as still underdeveloped beings in the course of becoming human. This viewpoint has been evident within traditional psychological and sociological perspectives which construct children as incomplete, passive objects rather than active subjects. Child studies customarily describe children as shaped through development (nature) or social influences (nurture) in order to become something else, namely the completed adult. Lee (2001a) argues that human beings are only taken seriously when they are fully formed and the fact that they are not yet adults is often used as a means for denying children full citizenship rights.

ACTIVITY 1

Do you agree that children are denied full citizenship rights?

Can you think of any examples of this?

One example of children's lack of citizenship rights is that they are an exception to the law that protects other citizens from violence. Physical punishment by parents, unlawful in many countries, is still legal in the UK under the defence of 'reasonable punishment' (section 58, Children Act 2004). It is a criminal offence to physically assault another adult but children still do not have the same protection under the law. However, the National Assembly of Wales has campaigned to outlaw smacking and there is a similar Scottish campaign called Children are Unbeatable.

Lee (2001a) suggests that the idea of children as incomplete adults necessitated the UN Convention on the Rights of the Child. Although there had been a Universal Declaration of Human Rights as far back as 1948, children were still excluded from many of these human rights until the UNCRC specifically stated that they should apply to children too.

This view of children as 'human becomings' values childhood primarily as the preparation for future adulthood. Prout argues that:

> A focus on futurity is unbalanced and needs to be accompanied by a concern for the present well-being of children, for their participation in social life and opportunities for human self-realisation.

(2000, p.305)

Such a discourse of futurity can be clearly seen in political rhetoric, particularly in relation to education and welfare policies. The powerful emotional resonance of this discourse for adults also leads to its use in advertising such as adverts for insurance which frequently use children as symbols of the future. This view positions children as objects of national investment – for instance, during the Depression of the 1930s the American president Herbert Hoover stated that 'Children are our most valuable natural resource'. Viewing children as a national resource rather than as individuals emphasises their future contribution and obscures the importance of children's present lives.

It is essential to recognise that childhood should be valued in its own right – not as preparation for something else which is to come. Recognition of children as independent beings, rather than as potential future adults, is a key Early Years principle (Bruce, 2005) and should underpin all practice with children.

ACTIVITY 2

Look through a range of media and collect items which refer to children and childhood. Try to find as wide a variety as you can – news stories, magazine features, advertisements, etc.

Sort through them and identify whose perspective is being used.

Are children's own views represented – or are they the views of adults about children?

Do you feel the children are represented as human beings – or as human becomings?

Children as social actors

Recognition of children as social beings in their own right led to what is generally termed the new social studies of childhood (see Chapter 1). After two decades, this perspective is no longer 'new' and it has now become commonplace to state that children are social actors (Prout, 2005). However, it is still important to understand the concepts of social actor and social agent and to recognise how these ideas link to wider debates about the place of childhood within society.

The idea of children as social actors began to emerge in the 1970s with the study of children's own perspectives on their lives. Recognition that children's voices had previously been treated as insignificant and therefore effectively *muted* (Hardman, 1973) underpinned studies of children's lives, revealing their potential to contribute to society rather than have other people speak on their behalf. As Prout and James put it *children must be seen as active in the construction and determination of their own social lives, the lives of those around them and of the societies in which they live* (1997, p.8).This crucial insight is fundamental to childhood studies, both as an academic discipline and in professional employment.

Berry Mayall develops this idea further and argues that children are not only social actors, but should be regarded as social agents. She describes the difference as follows:

> *A social actor does something … the term agent suggests a further dimension;*
> *negotiation with others, with the effect that the interaction makes a difference.*
>
> (2002, p.21)

The idea of *agency* is an important one in sociology and Mayall's emphasis on making a difference will be useful to bear in mind when we consider children's participation later in the chapter.

THEORY FOCUS

Structure and agency

Structure and agency are two key concepts of sociology; debates about whether social structures or individual agency determine people's lives have been fundamental to academic discussions of society for many years.

Structure refers to the social institutions and processes which make up any society, the *tangible mode of organisation which regulates both individual conduct and the patterns of interaction … between individuals* (James et al., 2001, p.200). Government, church, law and the family can all be regarded as structures and our lives are constrained by the particular features of these. For instance, one is obliged to obey the law or else suffer particular consequences. Chapter 3 considered how societies develop specific patterns of family life which strongly influence the experiences of both children and adults. Structure applies not only to these social institutions but also to the processes resulting from them and the expectations which determine how we behave. Therefore people's place within society (for instance their social class) will affect their behaviour and beliefs.

One of the criticisms of this view of society is that it is overly deterministic – that is, it suggests that people's lives are primarily determined by the social structures which surround them. The alternative perspective of *agency* lays more emphasis on people's ability to shape their own lives.

Agency focuses on people's capacity to act independently of these structures and to make their own social meanings. In this way society is understood as emerging from a set of practices which reproduce social behaviour; so individuals play a full role as autonomous participants in their social and cultural worlds.

Giddens (1984) has attempted to resolve the tension between these two opposing viewpoints by arguing that both agency and structure are important. His theory of *structuration* suggests that agency and structure should be seen as closely allied because not only do people's actions take place within social structures but these structures can also be challenged and transformed by people's actions.

The importance of structure and agency in the study of childhood is that *most questions raised about children's competencies, rights, responsibilities and needs have been located in the space between these poles* (James et al., 2001, p.202). In other words, these theoretical arguments are not just dry academic debates but are hugely significant for our understanding of the place of children within society. They form the conceptual background to our actions towards, and ideas about, real children.

To find out more about structure and agency and their impact on childhood see:

James, A, Jenks, C and Prout, A (2001) *Theorizing childhood*. Cambridge: Polity Press.

Children and competence

With the recognition of children as social agents has come acceptance of the need to listen to children and enable their participation in matters of direct concern to them. Although the academic study of childhood now recognises children's agency and the participation of children is written into many policies and frameworks, children are evidently subordinate in status to adults. Adults have more resources and authority and therefore have power over children's lives – as Scraton states *adults direct and children obey* (2004, p.163). This has led some writers (Oakley, 1994; James et al., 2001) to suggest that children actually hold 'minority status' within society and, despite holding certain rights, are widely excluded from public life.

ACTIVITY 3

You may or may not agree that children constitute a minority group.

Discuss this with a group of your peers and consider the implications for responding to children as social agents.

Do you think children are sufficiently capable to make decisions about their lives?

Is this a question of appropriate skills? Does it depend on the child's knowledge? Or is it a matter of sufficient experience?

To what extent is it age dependent?

How much do you think children can contribute to decisions about matters which affect their lives – for instance, what to eat and drink, the activities they participate in or where and with whom they live?

Are your views based on the nature of the decision, or the age of the child?

Do you feel there is an age before which children should not be allowed to have a say?

Is this because of their understanding of the issues? Or is it to do with difficulties regarding communication (for instance, some people believe that babies are too young to make their views heard).

Most of the concerns about children's participation revolve around the issue of *competence*. Ideas of whether children have the ability or suitable experience to make legitimate decisions are open to challenge from their adult caretakers. Although Article 12 of the UNCRC specifically states children's right to participate in decisions affecting their lives, it is not specific in terms of what this means in practice. There is no clear indication of precisely what might be understood by participation, nor of how it should occur. Another difficulty lies in the declaration that due consideration should be given to the child's age and maturity. There is no clear guidance about how this should be interpreted and no indication is given on how to gauge competence or who should make this judgement. It is implicit, though, that this will be the decision of an adult.

THEORY FOCUS

Article 12 of the UNCRC

1. *States parties shall assure to the child who is capable of forming his or her own views the right to express those views freely in all matters affecting the child, the view of the child being given due weight in accordance with the age and maturity of the child.*

2. *For this purpose, the child shall in particular be provided with the opportunity to be heard in any judicial and administrative proceedings affecting the child, either directly or through a representative or an appropriate body, in a manner consistent with the procedural rules of national law.*

See Chapter 7, page 88 for more detail about the UNCRC.

Chapter 1 explored the many contradictions that arise from legal definitions of childhood and so it is hardly surprising that assessing a child's competence is no simple matter. However, this is an instance where you might agree with Nick Lee that the view of children as human becomings (Lee, 2001a) denies them rights that are taken for granted by adults. Adults are free to make hundreds of decisions about their lives every day, ranging from the trivial to the highly significant, without needing to demonstrate their competence. Indeed if there were a general measure of competence it is likely that many adults might fail such a test. Everybody varies in the level of competence they may display at any given time and we all have experienced situations where we are more or less competent than at other times. As Hutchby and Moran Ellis argue, competence is not something one can 'possess' but is:

> ... an intrinsically contextual matter. Competence cannot be separated from the structural contexts within which it is displayed or negotiated.

> (1998, p.16)

This suggests that competence should not be seen as a matter of development increasing incrementally with age, but instead we must recognise that children need opportunities to practise and develop competence (Leverett, 2008b). Practitioners who respect children recognise how proficient they are from a very early age at expressing their views and making judgements when given the opportunity to do so. However, Lansdown (2005) points out how adults routinely underestimate children's competence. She makes the uncompromising suggestion that competency should be assumed unless adults are able to actively demonstrate to the contrary that children lack competence. Such a move might overcome the misleading confusion between competency and development whereby, as James and James (2008) point out, age is often used as a proxy for competence. They emphasise the importance of clarifying the distinction between the two.

Perhaps the reason that adults have traditionally been so reluctant to attribute competency to the child is because frequently expectations of children are so low. Assumptions about what children can and cannot do reinforce ideas of dependency and vulnerability. Developmental paradigms against which children are measured stress their immaturity and draw attention to their lack of development and what they are unable to do, rather than focusing on what they accomplish and contribute (Alderson, 2005).

Handley (2009) suggests that one of the reasons that participation rights have had limited effectiveness is because there is a tension between these and the child's right to protection, also laid down in the UN. The protection of vulnerable children fits much more easily alongside dominant constructions of childhood and is therefore more likely to govern adults' actions. What Lahman refers to as *the seemingly incompatible images of the* vulnerable *child and the* competent *child* (2008, p.284, original emphases) muddies the water because we are used to thinking of children as dependent on adults. Vulnerability and dependency imply that children are incomplete – still human becomings – and therefore lack the ability to contribute meaningfully to society. The conflict and tension between these two discourses of childhood leaves a 'gap' for interpretation so that the end result is that much of children's participation is merely tokenistic and pays lip-service to the idea.

The child who is capable of making valid decisions is difficult to reconcile with the weak and vulnerable child in need of protection but, as Jenks (1996) points out, much of the time what we call care can actually *enforce dependence* on children. This is particularly true in developed countries where extended education and a high level of prosperity collude to keep children dependent on their parents for much longer than is usual in other parts of the world.

Dependence need not necessarily be the same thing as helplessness and passivity as Alanen (cited in Mayall, 2002) demonstrated in her research among Finnish children. In Finland schools are closed one day a week and it is taken for granted by parents that their children will therefore be at home on their own or playing out with their friends unsupervised. However, children are trusted to be able to look after themselves competently and are not perceived, by themselves or by adults, as in constant need of regulation. This illustrates how it is our construction of childhood that determines the way we understand children and their capabilities. Children who are given responsibilities can demonstrate high levels of competence, frequently beyond the expectations of adults. Moss and Petrie suggest that instead of passive dependants, we should view children as *rich in potential, strong, powerful and competent* (2002, p.5).

Listening to children

The enhanced status of children whereby they are now recognised as active social agents means that children should be regarded as service users and stakeholders in their own right. Children's involvement and input should help make services more effective in meeting their needs than previously, when they were viewed as passive dependants and parents accessed services on their behalf (Moss and Petrie, 2002). Government commitment to listening to the views of children has been evident in most recent policy making; for instance, national consultation with children fed into the green paper *Every Child Matters* and the subsequent legislation (DfES, 2004b) states that children's views must be taken into account when designing services to meet their needs. Similarly the EYFS (DfES, 2007) specifically requires practitioners to listen to children as well as their parents and carers. Other initiatives have taken place on more local levels such as when children helped to conduct a survey which informed the Mayor of London's Children's Strategy (Hood, 2001), and the Children and Young People's Assembly of Wales (www.funkydragon.org) which enables children to share their concerns with ministers. Participation can be identified on a range of different levels (Alderson, 2000) from the individual setting to international initiatives working with bodies like the United Nations and NGOs such as charities. In this way children's voices have been effective in, among other issues, drawing attention to the problems of HIV/AIDS in Africa and campaigning on environmental issues (John, 2003). But arguably, the most important place to develop greater participation is at a local level where children can be involved in decision making about the day-to-day running of their schools, nurseries and other settings. This is more likely to prevent children's participation from being reduced to one-off tokenistic events rather than genuine democratic partnership.

The large-scale increase in initiatives which recognise children's agency (described by John (2003) as a *growth industry*) gives official endorsement to listening to children, but this is not enough on its own. Roberts (2008) has pointed out that just because there is greater consultation with children about policies which affect them, this does not mean that their views are necessarily heard. He draws attention to the difference between listening, hearing and actually acting on children's views and suggests that this last is the most difficult to bring about. Consultation may be used as window dressing for adult-led policies and lead to a very limited model of participation. Genuine participation requires taking children's views seriously. Commitment to children's input into decision-making processes can be a real challenge to many adults. It requires relinquishing control and authority which can seem like a threat to adults who are used to being in charge. It does not, however, mean simply handing over decision making to children so that they are in charge instead; meaningful participation requires a genuine collaborative relationship which respects other parties as equal partners. It is important too to include feedback loops so that children are aware of how their views have been listened to. This can also help to check that adults have properly understood what children mean and have not simply misinterpreted their views according to their own assumptions (Lancaster and Broadbent, 2003).

Another issue is that participation is frequently seen as something for older children and younger ones are deemed incapable of expressing their views. However young they are, children have views and opinions and these should not be overlooked or brushed aside simply because of their age (Alderson, 2000). Children, including the youngest babies, are competent to express their views in a range of different ways and respect for the child requires that we take account of these *hundred languages of childhood* (Malaguzzi, 1996) and make a point of finding ways to listen to and respond to the child's view. This may be more demanding in certain circumstances and need particular approaches and strategies, particularly in the case of preverbal children and those with special needs. However, this is not an excuse to ignore the voice of any child; the most important element is the commitment of the adults involved. Lancaster suggests that we need to actively create a *culture of listening* (2006) so that it becomes second nature to *pull up a chair* for the child in everything that we do.

It can be seen that participation may mean different things to different people and can be understood on a number of different levels. A useful model of participation to make sense of these varying interpretations has been developed by Roger Hart in the form of a ladder (1992, see Figure 3). Although there have been a number of criticisms of this model, it provides a helpful way of thinking about engaging with children and ranges from the superficial and meaningless steps, which Hart explains are not participation at all, through to genuine collaboration.

Hart's ladder has been criticised for a number of reasons. Firstly, it can be seen as a hierarchy whereby progress is made up the ladder and each additional step is an advance. It is better to consider the model as a continuum from which to select the most appropriate approach. For instance, there are situations (such as school) where children can never have control and therefore would never be able to reach the higher levels. Secondly, it might be interpreted as implying that adults 'give' the right to participate to children, and therefore to some extent still remain the ultimate authority. It is also important to remember that children, like adults, cannot be regarded as a heterogeneous group and to respect the fact that not all children will want to play an active role in participation. Another issue of debate regards the two highest levels: rung 7 where children lead and initiate action and rung 8 where they share decision making with adults.

Controversy centres around which of these levels is the most meaningful. Some people believe that shared decision making where power is distributed equally among children and adults is more important, whereas others feel that children are best empowered by enabling them to make decisions on their own where the adults' role is one of support. This again is a problem with viewing the ladder as a hierarchical model which implies that one of these ways of working is intrinsically better than the other, and can be best overcome by identifying the most appropriate approach for the circumstances. Leverett (2008b) suggests that Hart's ladder is particularly useful as a reminder to adults of how easy it is to get this wrong.

8 - child-initiated, shared decision making with adults	• Projects stem from children's ideas but decision making is shared equally between children and adults.
7 - child-initiated and directed	• Projects are developed and initiated by children and adults are only there to support if asked
6 – adult-initiated, shared decision making with children	• The initial idea comes from adults but all decision making is shared with the children
5 - children are consulted and informed	• Children are consulted on projects run by adults and their views are taken seriously
4 - children are assigned but informed	• Children are assigned roles in projects run by adults. Their views are taken seriously and they are made aware of why they have been involved
3 - tokenism	• Children are asked about their views but they have little impact on issues or choice about how they are involved
2 - decoration	• Children are used to illustrate an issue but have no understanding of the background or context
1 - manipulation	• Children are told what to say or do by adults to support adult-initiated projects

Figure 3 Hart's ladder of participation (adapted from Hart, 1992)

ACTIVITY 4

Consider Hart's ladder of participation in relation to your own practice and practice you have observed.

Think about examples of children's involvement and use the ladder to evaluate how much choice and autonomy children actually had.

Can you think of examples of the children's ideas and initiatives being acted on?

Or are they mainly adults' ideas in which children have an opportunity to be involved?

ACTIVITY *continued*

How often are children involved in activities and experiences which they do not understand and which are fairly meaningless to them?

What examples of adults and children working together in partnership can you identify?

What is your own view about the relative merits of the top two rungs of the ladder?

Examples of meaningful participation

The problems that have been identified in making participation a reality and the many hurdles which get in the way are daunting to practitioners wanting to make changes. However, there are many examples of creative and collaborative partnerships between adults and children which serve as an inspiring counterbalance.

- Children were actively involved in developing their Children's Centre garden. Children designed gardens in the sand tray and built a three-dimensional model with salt dough. They took part in discussions to develop ideas, consulted seed catalogues and used digital cameras to record good and bad features of the current outdoor space and evaluated these with happy and sad faces. The finished result was the result of the children's own ideas and their genuine contribution had been valued (Lancaster and Broadbent, 2003).

- Children's understanding of the unwritten ground rules of their setting were ascertained by introducing two dolls who were 'starting nursery today'. Children were asked to show the dolls what they needed to know. What the children revealed as important to understand was recorded and at the end of the week practitioners were surprised to realise how many 'ground rules', hitherto unspecified, the children had identified. (Lancaster, 2006)

- Children acted as inspectors in one first school where a group of children observed lessons and surveyed other children and parents. They then wrote reports which were shared with governors, staff, pupils and parents as a basis for improving provision (Save the Children, 2006; cited in Leverett, 2008b).

- On a run-down housing estate, a group of children aged between three and eight years old wrote a report for the council including photos, maps and drawings and based on their survey of other children's views. After meeting with senior officials they succeeded in getting plans for the play area changed to better meet the needs of the children (Newson, 1995; cited in Alderson, 2005).

There are many other examples of excellent practice like this (see the further reading suggestions on page 105) and Mooney and Blackburn (2003) argue that identifying children's views of their provision in this way can provide the most effective base for improving quality (cited in Leverett, 2008b).

These examples also demonstrate how children's voices have become more evident within research. Whereas, in the past, research on children's lives was carried out by adults, children as young as three are now routinely involved as research partners (Alderson, 2005). Research methodologies such as the Mosaic approach (Clark and Moss, 2001) enable children to evaluate their environment through models, digital photography and drawings so that even the youngest children can be actively involved. The *Children 5–16: growing into the Twenty-First Century* project run by the Economic and Social Research Council is also an excellent example of research carried out *with* children rather than *on* them. The children's input enabled insights into their perspectives which would never have been available to adults acting on their own.

However, the increasing involvement of children in research raises a variety of ethical considerations. It should be obvious that researchers must demonstrate respect for children, upholding their dignity as human beings in the same way as for adult participants. However, this has frequently not been the case and children are often seen as being too young to give informed consent. As a result, their own views on involvement may not be sought and parental consent has often been considered an adequate substitute. Children's understanding is clearly more limited than adults' and so researchers must proceed with sensitivity and be aware of the effect of power differentials; children usually want to please adults and their ability to choose not to take part in, or to withdraw from, an adult's practice is usually limited. This is too extensive an area to explore here but for a thorough examination of the issues of doing ethical research with children see Farrell (2005).

Finally, it is important that we do not lose sight of the real purpose of participation. Children are key stakeholders in any setting which they attend, or service which they access. Leverett (2008b) draws attention to the danger of participation as an end in itself rather than as a means to an end; in other words, situations where adults participate with children in order to meet their own agendas and demonstrate that they are doing so, rather than through a genuine desire to hear and act on children's views. Handley (2009) claims that children's views are less likely to be given consideration when they are at odds with those of their adult caretakers, which is a timely reminder that being prepared not simply to listen, but to actively *hear*, is fundamental to good practice.

ACTIVITY 5

Think about a child or group of children you have regular contact with. Consider recent decisions you have made in relation to them.

Are there times when you have made decisions for the children instead of with them?

Are there decisions that the children are able to make by themselves?

How can you work to ensure that children are able to fully participate in matters pertaining to their daily lives?

How can you develop a listening culture and adapt policies and practices to facilitate this? How will you ensure that you always pull up a chair (Lancaster, 2006) for the child?

Finally, if you are involved in research about young children's lives, consider ways in which you can involve them as research partners.

SUMMARY

This chapter has considered how attitudes towards children have changed in the past couple of decades and the implications of this for their actual lives. Traditional views of children as 'other' customarily led to them being excluded from normal social action while their lives were governed by adults. Recent sociological studies now recognise children as human beings in their own right rather than incomplete and underdeveloped 'human becomings' (Lee, 2001a). As a result of this new-found respect for children as social agents who actively construct their own life and make a difference to their environment, there has been a greater emphasis on children's participation. This ranges from government and local authority consultation with children about policies which will affect them to children's own input into everyday decision making in their settings. Although making participation meaningful can represent a serious challenge to adults, there are many examples of children's skills and aptitudes being recognised and their contributions welcomed in genuine collaborative partnerships.

FURTHER READING

Alderson, P (2000) *Young children's rights: exploring beliefs, principles and practice.* 2nd edition. London: Jessica Kingsley.

A very accessible account of how to pay attention to the rights of young children in everyday practice.

Clark, A, Kjørtholt, AT and Moss, P (eds) (2005) *Beyond listening: children's perspectives on early childhood services.* Bristol: The Policy Press.

A collection of approaches to 'listening as a pedagogy' from the UK, Scandinavia and Italy.

Handley, G (2009) Children's rights to participation, in Waller, T (ed) *An introduction to early childhood.* 2nd edition. London: Sage.

A straightforward explanation of the tensions that can arise between children's rights to participation and their competing rights to protection.

Lancaster, YP (2010) Listening to young children, in Pugh, G and Duffy, B (eds) *Contemporary issues in the Early Years.* 5th edition. London: Sage.

This chapter explores the issue of listening to children in relation to matters arising from the UNCRC and Every Child Matters. It includes a number of examples of meaningful listening from Kirklees Early Years Services.

Lancaster, YP and Broadbent, V (2003) *Listening to young children.* Maidenhead: Open University Press/McGraw-Hill Education.

An interdisciplinary resource based on the Coram Family's Listening to Young Children Project which supports practitioners in putting their commitment to young children's participation into practice.

Leverett, S (2008) Children's participation, in Foley, P and Leverett, S (eds) *Connecting with Children: developing working relationships.* Bristol: The Policy Press.

A very helpful guide to the theory and philosophy of participation, this chapter (and indeed the whole book) includes the voices of children in order to access their views and share their perspective.

WEBSITES

www.crae.org.uk
Children's Rights Alliance for England.

www.hull.ac.uk/children5to16programme
The Economic and Social Research Council's 'Children 5–16: Growing into the Twenty-First Century' project.

www.freechild.org
The Free Child Project exists to advocate for children and involve them in democratic action.

9 The twenty-first century child

Through reading this chapter, you will:

- consider arguments which have been raised about the 'disappearance' of childhood and evaluate the extent to which such claims are valid;
- increase your awareness of some of the factors which underpin supposed threats to childhood and children;
- understand how perceived vulnerability positions children as either victims or threats;
- examine the implications of these discourses for children's lives in the twenty-first century.

Childhood has always been *a site of adult anxiety* (Jenks, 1996, p.124), but the twenty-first century has seen an unprecedented rise in concern about children and the idea that childhood is becoming increasingly *toxic* (Palmer, 2006). This argument has been applied both to the social category of childhood as well as to worries about children themselves, who are perceived to be at risk of all sorts of damage inflicted by contemporary life. Evidence of the extent to which such anxieties have entered the social mainstream can be seen in the numbers of books published for the popular market in recent years. These all draw attention to the countless ways in which childhood is deteriorating, the perceived dangers facing modern children and the action adults should take in response (for example, Brooks, 2006; Palmer, 2006; Gill, 2007; Louv, 2008).

Media stories which focus on childhood in almost entirely negative ways stoke these concerns and breed unease and panic. In addition two recent reports on the material circumstances and well-being of children were widely publicised in the media. The UNICEF (2007) overview of child well-being in rich countries rated UK children the lowest of all 21 countries for both relationships and happiness. In terms of poverty, British children were fourth from the bottom and only one point above for educational well-being. The Good Childhood Inquiry (Children's Society, 2007) echoed concerns about relationships and friendships, highlighting the extent to which parental fears curtail children's freedom to play outside and raising issues about the commercialisation of modern childhood. Newspaper reporting which ignores context and other mitigating factors can therefore give the impression that childhood is under serious threat. Indeed, Brooks suggests that:

> Childhood has become the crucible into which is ground each and every adult anxiety … This is a time of child-panic.

(2006, p.16)

ACTIVITY **1**

Using a large sheet of paper, create a mind map of the contemporary child.

Try to identify the issues which cause unease and alarm among adults.

Look at these carefully and see if there are any connections or contradictions between the different ideas you have noted.

Are any of them related to particular groups of children? For instance, do issues of class, gender or background make any difference?

Keep your mind map so that you can refer back to it later after you have finished reading this chapter.

The disappearance of childhood?

One of the prime anxieties about contemporary childhood is that children grow up too quickly. This complaint is frequently heard from adults despite the fact that children remain dependent on their parents for a much longer period than they ever did in the past. From this perspective it could be argued that in reality childhood has been prolonged. Nonetheless, the *perception* remains that children, once deemed innocent and content to remain in their childish domain, are now in a hurry to rush into the world of adults. The popular appeal of such a viewpoint is mainly focused on the influence and effects of modern media. However, unease about increasing pressure on children within the education system reinforces these notions as well as disquiet about certain cultural changes such as the changing relationships between parents and children.

The most extreme position from this perspective is that children grow up so fast that childhood can no longer be said to really exist anymore. This is the argument which Postman (1994) put forward when he suggested that childhood is actually disappearing. Chapter 2 considered Postman's ideas of how technology, in the form of the printing press, 'created' modern childhood. He has suggested that childhood is now disappearing as a result of another technological innovation – namely television.

Postman argued that the traditional boundaries between children and adults are being eroded with the effect that there no longer exists a clear distinction between the two. He laid the blame for this on television because, as a visual medium, it does not make complex demands on the mind or segregate its audience by age. Therefore children are exposed to the same knowledge and information as adults. Postman claimed that nowadays children are better informed but warned that *in having access to the previously hidden fruit of adult information, they are expelled from the garden of childhood,* (1994, p.97). He suggested that increasing crime rates, alcoholism, drug taking and sexual activity among children provide evidence of childhood's 'disappearance'.

Postman's view is now generally recognised as exaggerated by most commentators (for example, Buckingham, 2000; Prout, 2005) and there are a number of ways in which his evidence might be challenged. Claims about an increase in sexual activity, drug taking and alcohol consumption for instance, are difficult to substantiate as there are no statistics for valid comparison. Also public attitudes towards such issues have changed as awareness has increased – for instance, at one time children were routinely given gin or laudanum (opium dissolved in alcohol) as treatment for minor ailments. Crime figures can also be expected to consistently rise as recording becomes more systematic and new laws 'create' new crimes. So Postman's evidence is not as conclusive as he would have liked to think. Nonetheless, the idea that children 'grow up too fast' retains a hold on the popular imagination and adults continue to mourn the 'loss' of childhood.

ACTIVITY 2

Discuss the issue of 'disappearing' childhood with your peers.

What do you think of Postman's evidence for his claim?

Compare the lifestyle of a child you know well to your own experiences as a child.

Do you think it is reasonable to claim that children no longer experience childhood? Or are they just growing up in different circumstances?

Who is it who wants the child to remain 'childlike'? Why might this be?

The tendency to view childhood in such alarmist terms is primarily a result of the dominance of a romantic discourse of childhood, discussed in Chapter 2. This discourse positions children as innocent and vulnerable; the consequence being that they must be sheltered from the dangerous adult world. Up until the middle of the twentieth century, for many children the actual experience of childhood began to resemble this romantic ideal more and more, perhaps best illustrated by the optimistic, post-war model of childhood in the 1950s. However, the alternative discourse, which views children as unruly and in need of adult control, is also still very prevalent in contemporary society and together these two viewpoints influence and shape public perceptions. As a result, children are primarily viewed as either victims in need of protection or else as threats to the social order. Indeed Hendrick (1994) suggests that within public debate there are only three possible roles for children who are constructed as victim, threat or national investment.

Children as victims

The debate about children growing up too fast actually hides deeper anxieties about sexuality and consumerism. In the past when families lived in more crowded conditions, children were aware of the facts of life – and death – from an early age. More recently, greater prosperity and smaller families have increased privacy, enabling adults to shield children from such realities and create the state of innocence that has come to be associated with 'proper' childhood. Concerns about sexuality are focused on a variety of issues including little girls wearing 'sexually explicit' clothing, sex education and moral panic about teenage pregnancy. These issues are all connected to the underlying assumption that childhood and sexuality must be mutually exclusive categories.

The idea that there is little difference between children's and adults' clothing is part of Postman's 'evidence' that childhood is disappearing. He suggested that as childhood and adulthood merge the 'symbolic markers' of childhood are reduced. In reality there was only ever a short period of time when children's clothes specifically set them apart from adults so that, for instance, little boys wore short trousers; through much of history children's clothes were simply smaller versions of their parents'. It is certainly true that contemporary fashion favours extremely short skirts and garments which reveal a lot of flesh. But it is an adult rather than a child's viewpoint that interprets these as sexual. Children do not grow up in a social vacuum and so in a celebrity-obsessed culture where sex is blatantly used to sell personalities as well as products, it is to be expected that little girls will want to copy what they see their role models wearing. This is not the same thing as sexual intent. It is adults' desire to keep children apart from the adult world which creates anxiety.

This was not always the case and children's knowledge of sexual matters would once have been treated in a much more matter of fact manner; social customs and culture determine what is considered appropriate in any given society and considerable variation exists (Kehily and Montgomery, 2004). For instance, the age at which it is deemed fitting to give birth has gradually been pushed later as childhood has been extended. Historically it was not unusual for girls to marry and have children from the age of 12 but by the twentieth century custom and legislation had moved this on to the late teens. Since the 1980s increased education and employment opportunities for women have resulted in most people delaying pregnancy until at least a decade later. Thus girls who go against expectations and continue to have babies before the social norm are seen as a problem, especially since the extension of childhood means they are now often regarded as still children themselves. So the ideal of childhood innocence is sustained by adults who police and control children's sexuality (Kehily and Montgomery, 2004). This causes problems for teachers and others who are expected to educate children about matters of sexuality but are at risk of having their professionalism questioned if they attempt to answer children's concerns and queries (Corteen and Scraton, 2004). In particular, anxiety about the 'promotion' of homosexuality has created considerable media commotion.

Children are also seen as potential victims in relation to consumerism. In an increasingly materialistic society, children are an important part of the economy and the huge market of material goods for children acts as a powerful incentive for parents to work and earn money (Leach, 1994); for instance, in January 2009 the Insurance group Liverpool Victoria estimated the cost of having a baby as £194,000. In marketing terms children also form an important demographic in their own terms. While the average income has doubled since the 1970s, children's pocket money is now ten times higher than it then was (Wall's Pocket Money Monitor, cited in John, 2003) and therefore the child market is a lucrative one. Children's 'pester power' is well recognised and they increasingly influence family expenditure on such things as holidays, car purchasing and eating out. All of this makes the child consumer an attractive target for manufacturers so that there is concern that children are *conscripted into consumption* at an early age (John, 2003, p.129). However, Karpf (2003, p.7) reminds us that these are *problems of affluence*. The increasing emphasis on spending and consumption creates different problems for poorer segments of society (see Chapter 5 for more about how poverty affects children's lives).

In response to inflated anxieties about marketing to children, Buckingham (1994) reminds us that children are more sophisticated than they are usually given credit for and should not be seen as the naïve and passive dupes of advertisers. Elsewhere he warns of the dangers of trying to position children in some kind of golden age where culture was not contaminated by commerce.

> *The notion that children should be somehow shielded from the influence of the market, in a 'pure', non-commercial sphere, is not only utopian; it also fails to provide a basis for equipping them to deal with the challenges of an increasingly market-oriented culture.*
>
> Buckingham (2004, p.116)

Children pick up the norms and values of the society they grow up in and in the twenty-first century adults place great store on material possessions, demonstrating their personal identity and social acceptability through what they own. However, children are criticised if they follow this example and considered to be materialistic and acquisitive (Robb, 2001). In the modern world there is a tension between adults' idealisation of childhood and the actual experience of children living in advanced capitalist societies; the discourse of innocence conflicts with discourses of consumerism and it is difficult to reconcile the image of the materialist child with the romantic view of childhood. So it can be seen that anxieties about children are frequently concerns about wider society which are projected onto children and the state of childhood. Because of children's association with the future, worries about an uncertain future often become worries about childhood and create moral panics.

THEORY FOCUS

Moral panic

Moral panic was a term coined by the sociologist Stanley Cohen who studied Mods and Rockers, youth cultures which emerged in the 1960s. He used the phrase to describe the way in which certain issues get taken up by the public at particular times and result in *sudden and overwhelming fear and anxiety*. Cohen pointed out that, due to the amount of attention focused on the issue, the level of hysteria is considerably in excess of the actual threat which is posed.

Cohen described the development of a moral panic as follows:

> *A condition, episode, person or group of persons emerges to become defined as a threat to societal values and interests; its nature is presented in stylised and stereotypical fashion by the mass media; the moral barricades are manned by editors, bishops, politicians and other right-thinking people; socially accredited experts pronounce their diagnoses and solutions; ways of coping are evolved or (more often) resorted to; the condition then disappears, submerges or deteriorates and becomes less visible.*
>
> (1987, p.9)

Cohen termed such groups or individuals *folk devils*, by which he meant those who become the focus of public fear and apprehension as *visible reminders of what we should not be*. Subsequent youth identities which could be described in the same way were

continued

hippies, punks and goths and similar concerns can be discerned in public debate about rave culture, hip hop and 'hoodies'.

Childhood is an area particularly prone to this kind of overreaction and there have been many moral panics relating to children's leisure pursuits and play, such as excessive alarm about Power Rangers and Pokémon. In particular, moral panic can be identified in connection with many aspects of technology, especially video games.

ACTIVITY 3

To what extent can current concerns about childhood obesity be considered as a moral panic?

Look through Cohen's description of a moral panic (above) and see how much of it you are able to apply to public reaction to childhood obesity.

What do you think David Buckingham means when he suggests that fat children have become a new kind of folk devil in contemporary society (Buckingham, 2005)?

Obesity is another of the ways in which children are deemed to be in danger from the modern world. In actual fact, children are generally healthier and have more varied diets than at any time in history. The easy availability of cheap food and ready prepared meals does not promote health and there are undeniably children who are considerably overweight; however, panics about the state of children's health are often unfounded or exaggerated (Guldberg, 2009). Obesity is generally connected to poverty and a focus on childhood obesity can obscure the real underlying social issues which need to be addressed. In reality awareness of healthy eating has never been higher and reflects a cultural obsession with the body and physical appearance as well as an overwhelming anxiety about food in general.

Children as threats

One of the problems of viewing children as naturally pure and untarnished by society is that it rules out alternative perspectives of 'normal' children. Adults create an unrealistic model of childhood and then children who do not conform to this are labelled as problems, deviant and a threat to the social order. This is particularly the case in relation to children living in poverty who are frequently portrayed as part of a dysfunctional underclass so that certain children come to be ascribed 'demon' status (Goldson, 2001). Cases of children's involvement in crime, whether as victims or perpetrators, are over-reported in the media when compared to adult crime. Stories are distorted and their significance exaggerated, creating and reinforcing negative perceptions of childhood. The Good Childhood Inquiry recognised this tendency in stating that:

A brief scan of recent headlines in the UK press quickly illustrates our contradictory and dichotomous attitudes towards children and young people: our angels or demons, innocents or deviants.

(Children's Society, 2007, p.6)

ACTIVITY 4

Headliners, a young people's media group, studied portrayals of children in the press and identified seven different categories through which children are commonly described and understood. They found that children are usually portrayed as stereotypes such as victims, angels or little devils.

Collect as many stories as you can from a variety of newspapers that concern children. Make sure you include both tabloids and broadsheet papers.

Analyse how the children are depicted. Consider the way that language is used, such as the choice of particular words and phrases, as well as pictures.

What sort of categories can you identify?

How does media coverage of children create or reinforce public perceptions of children?

What do these representations reveal about attitudes towards children in modern society?

Although you can do this as an individual, you are likely to find more variety if you work as part of a group. This also enables you to discuss your ideas with others.

You can read the full report at:

www.headliners.org/storylibrary/stories/1998/thesevendeadlystereo types/htm

---

An additional aspect of media accounts of children 'out of control' and 'persistent young offenders' is that there is an implication that this behaviour is indicative of all children. News stories about adults treat criminals as individual wrong-doers, but press coverage of children in trouble with the law suggests that an entire generation is morally degenerate (Davis and Bourhill, 2004). The result of this is an increasing public fear of children and what Scraton has termed *the ideological whiff of child hate* (cited in Goldson, 2001).

Public outrage at the apparent waywardness of modern children brings calls for ever more repressive measures of control and punishment. The UN Committee on the Rights of the Child has expressed criticism of the young age at which children enter the criminal justice system in the UK. It is argued that this cannot be in their best interests and that children who break the law should be regarded as a social rather than a criminal problem. The age of criminal responsibility in England, Wales and Northern Ireland is ten which is the lowest in Europe. Until 2009 this had been even younger in Scotland when it was raised from eight to 12 to bring legislation more in line with other countries. Duncan Campbell and Alan Travis (2007) point out the differences in approaches to children who offend:

The last three years has seen a 26 per cent increase in the numbers of children and young people criminalised and seven times as much is spent on youth custody as on prevention schemes. We lock up 23 children per 100,000 of the population, compared to six in France, two in Spain, 0.2 in Finland.

(The Guardian, 2007, p.12)

The repercussions of such punitive attitudes affect all children and trickle down to the very youngest. The boundaries of 'normality' have been reduced so that what was once perceived as youthful high spirits or childish naughtiness, only to be expected in the young, is now often viewed as problem behaviour and an indication of later delinquency.

Perceptions of children as victims or threats are highly gendered; anxieties about sexuality usually focus on girls – unless a boy is 'insufficiently' masculine and shows a particular interest in dressing up. In contrast, concerns about antisocial behaviour are primarily centred on boys and there have been cases of small boys excluded from nurseries and labelled as future delinquents before they even reach the school system. Class is also a factor; a group of young males running around may be interpreted as youthful high spirits if they are pupils of a highly regarded public school yet be seen as a sign of impending depravity if lower-class boys in an inner city are involved. Historically, the children of the poor have always been regarded as a threat and subjected to measures to control them. Ignoring the socio-economic and class factors allows blame to be diverted away from society itself onto easy scapegoats such as single parents and 'video nasties'. Childhood is always mediated through class and gender and, in an increasingly multicultural society, ethnicity is also an important factor with black boys being at particular risk of being labelled as 'problems'.

The idea of children as threatening the social order does not prevent them from also being regarded as victims. James and James (2004) suggest that by constructing children as a threat to society and in need of social control, the child simultaneously becomes a vulnerable victim who needs care. So vulnerability is a concept that has now been extended to all children.

Children and technology

Of all the anxieties about modern children, one of the greatest centres on technology. Postman (1994) was not alone in worrying about the effects of television which is commonly supposed to endanger children's learning, physical well-being and ability to make relationships, although there is little empirical evidence to support these concerns (Guldberg, 2009). Technology naturally impacts on children's lives as it does on society as a whole and there is no reason to automatically assume that this impact must be a negative one. Nick Lee (2001b) suggests that a positive result of television's invasion of the home is that it acts as an 'extension' in bringing children into the public world and thus has been instrumental in the growing awareness of children as active social agents.

The introduction of any new cultural form has always raised alarm and similar panics can be identified historically in connection with cinema, comics and theatrical performances. However, because of the rapid rate of change since the introduction of new digital technologies, adults can feel especially anxious about their inability to control the environments of their children. Buckingham points out the similarity between adult fears about technology and children:

Like the idea of childhood itself, technology is often invested with our most intense fears and fantasies. It holds out the promise of a better future, while simultaneously provoking anxieties about a fundamental break with the past.

(2004, p.108)

These fears are made worse by the perception that children are more skilled and competent in their use of technology than adults, which holds an additional threat of reversing customary power relationships. Prensky (2001) has described children as digital natives, meaning that they were born and have grown up in an era of technology which they take for granted. Anyone born before the development of modern technology can be seen as a digital immigrant – living in a 'foreign' environment where the language and the culture need to be learned rather than simply assimilated. As digital natives children are able to competently negotiate a variety of textual practices as they move easily between printed, visual and electronic texts (Marsh, 2005).

Modern technologies are becoming more important in children's lives, not only because of the increasing dominance of technology in the modern world but also as parents increasingly invest in more and more entertainment media to keep their children safely at home in response to perceived dangers in the outside world (Hutchby and Moran Ellis, 2001). As the availability of new media technologies becomes ever greater there is a corresponding anxiety from adults who did not have such resources when they themselves were children. Computer games are frequently seen as a corrupting influence on children's behaviour and alongside television and DVDs are an easy target to blame for the supposed demise of childhood. Other concerns have been raised about the trivialisation of modern life and education where electronic media replace printed texts (Postman,1987,1994). On the other hand, some commentators have veered towards more utopian views of technology, such as Papert (1993) who claims 'the children's machine' (i.e. the computer) has transformed learning and Tapscott (1998) who suggests that the internet enables a new generation to be more creative, democratic and self-aware. Katz even suggests that:

Children can for the first time reach past the suffocating boundaries of social convention, past their elders' rigid notions of what is good for them.

(1997, p.174)

As Buckingham (2004) reminds us, both of these extremes are based on adult *images* of the child, whether as media-wise or vulnerable innocent, and it is important to take a more balanced view which moves beyond the belief that technology has consequences in itself outside the social contexts in which it operates.

Childhood in a risk-averse society

Despite the fact that we live in *an historically unheard of level of safety* (UNICEF, 2007, p.15), fears for the safety of children have never been higher. Parents' reluctance to let their children roam outdoors on their own was highlighted in the Good Childhood Inquiry (Layard and Dunn, 2009) and it is estimated that the average distance children can explore outdoors without an adult has shrunk by 90 per cent in the past 30 years (Brooks, 2006). The reality is that children today are no more at risk than in the past; child murders and abductions have not increased while roads have actually become safer (Midgley, 2006). In respect of traffic accidents, there has been a massive *decrease* of 75 per cent in child deaths since the 1970s while the number of child murders in England and Wales remains more or less constant at about 79 a year – very few of which happen at the hands of strangers (Gill, 2007). However, extensive media coverage of high-profile abductions, such as those of Holly Wells, Jessica Chapman and Madeleine McCann, with no mention of how rare such occurrences are, ensures that a culture of anxiety remains. Although increased media attention is largely a result of more news outlets including 24-hour news channels and the internet, the perception is that the danger itself has increased. Midgley (2006) cites a BBC poll which showed 76 per cent of Scottish parents believed child abductions had increased and 38 per cent thought this increase had been 'dramatic'. Acting on these distorted perceptions, parents are not prepared to risk letting their children out of their sight with the result that UK children have become 'hostages' to parental fears (Children's Society, 2007).

Considerable alarm has been raised about the implications for this generation of 'battery children' raised in captivity who Richard Louv suggests are suffering from *nature deficit disorder* (2008, p.10). Figures from the Department for Transport show that in 2006 only 5 per cent of children were allowed to travel to school unaccompanied, in comparison to 80 per cent in 1971 (DfT, 2007). This security culture has become so deeply embedded that we take it for granted that children's play should now be closely supervised so as to ensure complete safety at all times. Gill (2007) warns of the dangers of such a zero-risk approach and suggests that our determination to eliminate every conceivable danger ultimately puts children at greater risk because they are unable to judge situations for themselves. He refutes the idea that children are growing up too fast and believes that, in contrast, the long-term consequences of denying children responsibility is that they are infantilised.

Gill is not alone in his concerns about the over-protection of children in contemporary society and this growing disquiet is evident in the widespread use of metaphors such as cotton wool and bubble wrap. For instance, education minister Ed Balls pointed out that *we cannot wrap children in cotton wool – this is not protecting children* (Balls, 2007) and a recent Scottish campaign drawing attention to how child safety prevails over all other issues was called 'Cotton wool kids can't swim' (cited in Guldberg, 2009). The ability to judge risks is something that needs practice to acquire and even the Royal Society for the Prevention of Accidents warns of the danger of overprotection suggesting that we should be *as safe as necessary, not as safe as possible* (RoSPA, 2007, p.13).

As children's lives become increasingly structured and their free time scheduled by parents, there is a danger that adults' distorted perception of danger is projected onto children themselves. A number of surveys have found that children are becoming frightened to play outside by themselves and although they would like to spend more time outside, associate the outdoors with danger (see, for example, Thomas and Thompson, 2004).

Another aspect of living in *a culture that prizes 'safety' above all else* (Guldberg, 2009, p.2) is a remarkable growth in the surveillance of children's lives over the last couple of years. Modern technology has enabled the development of a whole range of devices for tracking children and these find a ready market from parents obsessed with their child's safety. It is now possible to buy teddy bears or other objects with built-in webcams to enable a vigilant parent to watch their child at any time of day or night. Electronic tags can be purchased to sew into clothes in the same way as a name tape. These react to sensors fitted on doors and windows to sound an alarm if the child moves outside the confines of the house. Many other devices to track or monitor a child's whereabouts are available which *feast on our fears* (Katz, 2005, p.108) and there are suggestions that implanted microchips might become as routine with children as they are with animals. In a recent report the thinktank Future Foundation found that many parents are enthusiastic about the development of such technology and 75 per cent would buy an electronic bracelet to track their child's movements if they could (Future Foundation, 2006). This concern to monitor children at all times even extends to the nursery or kindergarten with a growing number of settings installing webcams so parents can check on their children from home or work. A spokesman for Future Foundation said that today's generation is growing up used to the fact that *parents expect to know where they are at all times* (Atkins, 2005, p.1). The overriding concern to protect children is used as justification not simply to track children but also to monitor their activities. As the age that children have their own email accounts and mobile phones drops, many parents now believe it is acceptable to read children's emails and text messages (Guldberg, 2009). Such 'snooping' into a child's private life which would once have been considered unacceptable is now commonplace, raising concerns that the 'protection' of children has reached worryingly epic proportions and that children lack the privacy necessary for self-realisation and the development of lasting friendships with peers. The 'hypervigilance' (Katz, 2005) which causes adults to constantly intervene in children's lives has many implications for relationships and prolongs both physical and emotional dependence.

So is there a crisis in childhood?

The childhood of today's children is significantly different to that experienced by their parents and this makes adults feel very apprehensive. Jenks (1996) suggests that adults attempt to create 'yesterday's child' – in other words, they want to reproduce the circumstances of their own childhood. Such expectations inevitably lead to disenchantment with contemporary childhood and when such worries are amplified by the media, the result is a general concern about the state of modern childhood.

But are these concerns justified? Or are they perhaps the echoes of more general social anxieties that have emerged at the beginning of the twenty-first century? One of the themes of this book has been the location of the micro situation of the child's life within the wider macro circumstances (Bronfenbrenner, 1979). Taking that perspective it is clearly unrealistic, and inappropriate, to imagine that children's lives can remain frozen in some kind of timeless bubble outside of wider social changes. As Cunningham points out, there is *an increasing disjuncture between the romantic ideal and the lived reality* (1995, p.190).

However, it is probable that this 'disjuncture' has always existed. It is not unusual for the present to be compared unfavourably to the past because it is based on adults' nostalgia for their own childhoods. The following complaint is widely attributed to Socrates, a Greek philosopher writing in Athens in the fourth century BC.

> *The children now love luxury; they have bad manners, contempt for authority; they show disrespect for elders and love chatter in place of exercise. Children are now tyrants, not the servants of their households. They no longer rise when elders enter the room. They contradict their parents, chatter before company, gobble up dainties at the table, cross their legs, and tyrannize their teachers.*

This demonstrates that adult concern about the shortcomings of the younger generation is nothing new. Nostalgia for a supposed 'golden age' of childhood is the result of romantic positioning of the child based on a particular version of childhood. However, Marsh (2002) agues that in reality this ideal was only ever experienced by a middle-class minority. The actual lived experience of childhood for the majority has rarely measured up to the adult ideal.

Adults' perceptions of childhood are evident in the frequent use of the metaphor of a walled garden, a protected, lovely and natural place. Again, this is an adult perspective and it is important to recognise that it may not necessarily be shared by children. Holt (1975) argued that in practice the walled garden imprisons children within the state of childhood. He claimed that children are not naturally incompetent but are made so by adults' actions and so need to 'escape' from childhood. When one considers the ways in which modern childhood is restricted, supervised and controlled, it is possible to have considerable sympathy with this view.

Childhood does not take place within a social vacuum and the issues, concerns, problems and threats which are believed by many to besiege it need to be seen as part of the wider society and to reflect a broader cultural unease. In this way, Goldson argues that childhood can be seen as a *barometer of the nation* (2001, p.34).

Perhaps the 'problem' with modern childhood, if such a thing indeed exists, is that it is presented through the perceptions of adults. Children grow up in their own present and know no other world. This is their social context and it is important not to underestimate the ability of children to play an active role in their own lives. Cunningham points out how in the past children were assumed to have capabilities that we now rarely credit them with. While rejoicing in the fact that children no longer suffer the hardships and privations of the past, he warns of the dangers of overlooking their potential and their capabilities:

> *So fixated are we on giving our children a long and happy childhood that we downplay their abilities and their resilience. To think of children as potential victims in need of protection is a very modern outlook, and it probably does no-one a service.*
>
> (2006, p.245)

ACTIVITY 5

Look again at the mind map which you created for Activity 1 on page 108.

Is there anything you would now add or alter?

How many of these issues do you think are a real threat to modern childhood and how many are wider social issues which are projected on to childhood?

ACTIVITY *continued*

Do you think that some of these anxieties are possibly adult concerns rather than real dangers?

Remind yourself of Bronfenbrenner's model of child development in Chapter 1 (see page 13) and consider how the reality of childhood experience is created by the social systems in which it is embedded.

Finally, what is your own view of these issues?
Do you yourself think there is a crisis in regard to childhood in contemporary society?

SUMMARY

The twenty-first century is a time of anxiety and worries in relation to almost every aspect of modern life. Not surprisingly a lot of these fears coalesce around the topic of childhood. Modern children are widely thought to be at risk from multiple sources including crime, sexuality, consumerism, technology and even food. The objective reality is that much of this concern is inflated and exaggerated.

Childhood as a category of social analysis can never be entirely divorced from other variables such as class, gender and ethnicity and so current concerns about any 'crisis' facing childhood need to be interpreted with this in mind. Ideas of what is appropriate and acceptable vary and many wider social anxieties are projected on to childhood. When these concerns are amplified by the media the result is widespread moral panic about the state of childhood today.

Guldberg suggests that:

> *The crisis of childhood is caused less by the realities of the modern world than by an overly* negative *perception of the modern world ...*

> *(2009, p.179, original emphasis)*

Negative perceptions combined with greater economic prosperity have enabled the period of life regarded as childhood to be considerably extended. This has resulted in an over-protective attitude towards children – but such a risk-averse approach could be argued to create incompetence and dependency and to deny children's agency. It is therefore more important than ever that adults recognise and value children's abilities and potential.

FURTHER READING

Buckingham, D (2000) *After the death of childhood: growing up in the age of the electronic media.* Cambridge: Polity Press.

This is one of the most objective and helpful accounts of 'disappearing' childhood arguments. Buckingham gives a comprehensive and balanced account of media and childhood.

Buckingham, D (2004) New media, new childhoods? Children's changing cultural environment in the age of digital technology, in Kehily, MJ (ed) *An introduction to childhood studies.* Maidenhead: Open University Press/McGraw-Hill Education.

A short introduction to debates about children and technology that considers the ways in which children's lives have been shaped and changed by the new media age. Buckingham argues against both excessive anxiety and over-enthusiasm and instead calls for the relationship between childhood and technology to be set within its wider social context.

Foley, P, Roche, J and Tucker, S (eds) (2001) *Children in society: contemporary theory, policy and practice.* Basingstoke: Palgrave.

Essential reading to locate contemporary concerns about children's lives

Guldberg, H (2009) *Reclaiming childhood: freedom and play in an age of fear.* Abingdon: Routledge.

A very approachable book which examines the fears and uncertainties surrounding contemporary childhood and argues for a more balanced approach.

Scraton, P (ed) (2004) *'Childhood' in 'crisis'?* Abingdon: Routledge.

A wide-ranging book in which different authors examine a number of topics in relation to the perceived 'crisis' in childhood to consider how such concerns arise. Among other issues, chapters cover the role of the media, ways in which children are constructed as victims or threats and how childhood innocence is perceived and enforced.

WEBSITES

www.childrenssociety.org.uk
Website of the Children's Society.

www.childrenssociety.org.uk/all_about_us/how_we_do_it/the_good_childhood_inquiry/about_the_good_childhood_inquiry/2254.html
Direct link to *The Good Childhood Inquiry*.

www.fairplayforchildren.org
Campaigns for children's right to play and produces newsletters and downloadable information sheets on a wide range of topics.

Time line

1450	Invention of the printing press – over the next 50 years over 6,000 books printed
1552	Christ's Hospital founded in London
1601	The Elizabethan Poor Law enacted
1693	John Locke publishes *Some Thoughts Concerning Education*
1744	Thomas Corum's foundling hospital opened
1762	Jean-Jacques Rousseau publishes *Emile*
1819	Factory Act banned children under nine from working in textile mills but with no inspection to back up legislation
1833	Factory Act prohibited employment of under-nines in textile mills and regulated the hours of older children, supported by inspectors
1837	Registration of births made compulsory in England and Wales
1842	Mines Act prohibited children under ten from working underground
1855	Registration of births made compulsory in Scotland
1860	Children under 12 prohibited from working underground in mines
1864	Factory Act extended protection to children in other dangerous occupations
1864	Registration of births made compulsory in Ireland
1868	National Education League set up to campaign for elementary education
1870	Forster Education Act established school boards to set up schools where insufficient voluntary church schools existed
1870	Dr Barnardo set up his first children's home
1874	Factory Act, minimum working age of nine and limited hours for under-14s
1875	Chimney Sweeper Act banned climbing boys
1880	Education Act – schooling compulsory for children between five and ten
1884	National Society for the Prevention of Cruelty to Children founded
1891	Education Act made schooling free for all children
1891	Minimum working age for children in factories raised to 11
1893	School leaving age raised to 11
1899	School leaving age raised to 12

1906	Education Act brought in school dinners to improve children's health
1914–1918	First World War
1918	School leaving age raised to 14
1918	Women over the age of 30 given the vote
1922	The Republic of Ireland became an independent country
1928	Women given the same political rights as men
1939–1945	Second World War
1942	The Beveridge Report laid the foundations of the welfare state
1944	The Butler Education Act divided schools into primary and secondary and raised the school leaving age to 15
1948	The National Health Service came into existence
1961	The contraceptive pill first became available in Britain
1967	The Plowden Report on primary education recommended (limited) nursery provision
1967	The British Abortion Act legalised abortion (but did not apply to Northern Ireland)
1969	The Divorce Law Reform Act created a single ground for divorce (irretrievable breakdown of marriage)
1970	The Equal Pay Act
1973	School leaving age raised to 16
1975	The Sex Discrimination Act
1978	The Warnock Report reviewed educational provision for children with disabilities
1979–97	Conservative government in power
1981	Education Act created legislation to support recommendations of the Warnock Report; introduced concept of 'special educational needs'
1989	United Nations Convention on the Rights of the Child
1989	Children Act recognised the child as paramount
1990	The Rumbold Report recognised the importance of graduate practitioners
1996	*Desirable Outcomes for children's learning on entering compulsory education* published
1997	New Labour came to office

1998	The National Childcare Strategy published to support parents return to work; established Early Years Development and Childcare Partnerships
1998	Northern Ireland assembly set up to govern Northern Ireland
1999	The Scottish Executive and the National Assembly of Wales set up
2000	*Curriculum Guidance for the Foundation Stage* published
2001	Special Educational Needs and Disability Act revised Code of Practice for children with special educational needs
2001	Wales appointed a Children's Commissioner
2002	Sure Start Unit established
2002	*Birth to Three Matters* published
2003	*Laming Report* on death of Victoria Climbié
2003	*Every Child Matters* Green Paper published
2003	Children's Centres programme began
2003	Northern Ireland appointed a Children's Commissioner
2004	Children Act to legislate for *Every Child Matters*
2004	The *Ten Year Strategy for Childcare* published
2004	Scotland appointed a Children's Commissioner
2005	Children's Workforce Development Council established
2005	England appointed a Children's Commissioner
2005	Civic Partnership Act allowed same sex couples to wed
2006	Childcare Act legislation to support the *Ten Year Strategy*
2007	Unicef Report and Good Childhood Report both ranked welfare of children in Britain very low
2007	The Children's Plan developed in response to above reports
2008	Early Years Foundation Stage introduced in England
2008	Child Poverty Bill introduced to Parliament
2009	Single Equality Bill introduced to Parliament

References

Abbott, L and Nutbrown, C (eds) (2001) *Experiencing Reggio Emilia: implications for pre-school provision*. Buckingham: Open University Press.

Aiginger, K and Guger, A (2006) The European socioeconomic model, in Giddens, A, Diamond, P and Liddle, R (eds) *Global Europe, social Europe.* Cambridge: Polity Press.

Aitken, S and Jones, L (2005) Exploring families, in Jones, L, Holmes, R and Powell, J (eds) *Early childhood studies: a multiprofessional perspective.* Maidenhead: Open University Press/McGraw-Hill Education.

Alanen, L (1994) Gender and generation, in Qvortup, J, Bardy, M, Sgritta, G and Wintersberger, H (eds) *Childhood matters.* Aldershot: Avebury.

Alanen, L and Mayall, B (eds) (2001) *Conceptualising child–adult relations.* Abingdon: RoutledgeFalmer.

Alderson, P (2000) *Young children's rights: exploring beliefs, principles and practice.* 2nd edition. London: Jessica Kingsley.

Alderson, P (2005) Children's rights; a new approach to studying childhood, in Penn, H *Understanding Early childhood: issues and controversies.* Maidenhead; Open University Press/McGraw-Hill Education.

Ali, T (2009) No more Mr Nice Guy. *Guardian,* 31 October, p.4.

Alston, P (1994) *The best interests of the child: reconciling culture and human rights.* Oxford: Clarendon Press.

Archard, D (1993) *Children's rights and childhood.* London: Routledge.

Archard, D (2003) *Children, family and the state.* Aldershot: Ashgate.

Ariès, P (1986) *Centuries of childhood: a social history of family life.* London: Penguin Books.

Atkins, L (2005) Tagged, and ready for bed. *Guardian*, 3 December, p.1.

Aubrey, C (2010) Leading and working in multi-agency teams, in Pugh, G, and Duffy, B, (eds) *Contemporary issues in the Early Years.* 5th edition. London: Sage.

Baldock, P, Fitzgerald, D and Kay, J (2009) *Understanding Early Years policy.* 2nd edition. London: Sage.

Ball, SJ and Vincent, C (2005) The 'childcare champion'?: New Labour, social justice and the childcare market. *British Educational Research Journal,* 31(5): 557–70.

Balls, E (2007) 'Every Child Matters', speech to the National Children's Bureau at the launch of *Staying Safe*, 23 July.

Bayliss, J and Sly, F (2009) *Children and young people around the UK, regional trends 41.* London: Office for National Statistics available. Online at **www.statistics.gov.uk/regionaltrends41**.

Bennett, J (2003) Starting strong: the persistent division between care and education. *Journal of Early Childhood Research* 1(1): 21–48.

Bernardes, J (1997) *Family studies: an introduction.* London: Routledge.

Bourdieu, P and Passeron, JC (1990) *Reproduction in education, society and culture.* 2nd edition. London: Sage.

Boyden, J (1994) *The relationship between education and child work.* Child Rights Series no 9. Florence: Innocenti Research Centre.

Boyden, J (1997) Childhood and the policy makers: a comparative perspective on the globalisation of childhood, in James, A and Prout, A (eds) *Constructing and reconstructing childhood: contemporary issues in the sociological study of childhood*. 2nd edition. Lewes: Falmer Press.

Boyden, J, Ling, B and Myers, W (eds) (1998) *What works for working children?* Stockholm: Radda Barnen/UNICEF.

Brannen, J and Moss, P (eds) (2003) *Rethinking children's care.* Buckingham: Open University Press

Bronfenbrenner, U (1972) *Two worlds of childhood: US and USSR.* New York: Simon & Schuster.

Bronfenbrenner, U (1979) *The ecology of human development.* Cambridge, MA: Harvard University Press.

Bronfenbrenner, U (1986) Ecology of family as a context for human development: research perspectives. *Developmental Psychology.* 22: 723–42.

Brooks, L (2006) *The story of childhood: growing up in Modern Britain.* London: Bloomsbury.

Bruce, T (2005) *Early childhood education.* 3rd edition. London: Hodder Education.

Buckingham, D (1994) *Children talking television: the making of television literacy.* Lewes: Falmer Press.

Buckingham, D (2000) *After the death of childhood: growing up in the age of the electronic media.* Cambridge: Polity Press.

Buckingham, D (2004) New media, new childhoods? Children's changing cultural environment in the age of digital technology, in Kehily, MJ (ed) *An introduction to childhood studies.* Maidenhead: Open University Press/McGraw-Hill Education.

Buckingham, D (2005) Constructing the 'media competent' child: media literacy and regulatory policy in the UK. Medien Pädagogic Online. Available at **www.medienpaed.com/05-1/buckingham05-1.pdf**

Burr, R (2004) Children's rights: international policy and lived practice, in Kehily, MJ (ed) *An introduction to childhood studies.* Maidenhead: Open University Press/MacGraw-Hill Education.

Campbell, D and Travis, A (2007) UK headed for prison meltdown. *Guardian*, 31 March.

Central Advisory Council for Education (CACE) (1967) *Children and their primary schools (The Plowden Report).* London: HMSO.

Children's Society (2007) *The Good Childhood Inquiry.* London: The Children's Society.

Children's Workforce Development Council (CWDC) (2007) *The common assessment framework for children and young people: practitioner's guide: integrated working to improve outcomes for children and young people.* Leeds: CWDC.

Children's Workforce Development Council (CWDC) (2009) *Candidate's handbook: a guide to the gateway review and assessment process.* London: CWDC.

Chiosso, R (2008) The swings and roundabouts of community development, in Jones, P, Moss, D, Tomlinson, P and Welch, S (eds) *Childhood: services and provision for children.* Harlow: Pearson Longman.

Christenson, P and James, A (2008) *Research with children: perspectives and practice.* Abingdon: Falmer Press.

Clark, A and Moss, P (2001) *Listening to young children: the Mosaic Approach.* London: National Children's Bureau.

Clark, A, Kjørtholt, AT and Moss, P (2005) *Beyond listening: children's perspectives on early childhood services.* Bristol: The Policy Press.

Clark, MM and Waller, T (eds) (2007) *Early childhood education and care: policy and practice.* London: Sage.

Cohen, S (1987) *Folk devils and moral panics: the creation of the Mods and Rockers.* Oxford: Blackwell.

Coppock, V (2004) 'Families' in 'crisis'?, in Scraton, P (ed) *'Childhood' in 'crisis'?* Abingdon: Routledge.

Corteen, K and Scraton, P (2004) Prolonging 'childhood', manufacturing 'innocence' and regulating 'sexuality', in Scraton, P (ed) *'Crisis' in 'Childhood'?* Abingdon: Routledge.

Cunningham, H (1995) *Children and childhood in Western society since 1500.* London: Longman Group Ltd.

Cunningham, H (2003) Children's changing lives from 1800 to 2000, in Maybin, J and Woodhead, M (eds) *Childhoods in context.* Chichester: John Wiley & Sons and Open University Press.

Cunningham, H (2006) *The Invention of Childhood.* London: BBC Books.

Curriculum Review Programme Board (CRPB) (2006) *A curriculum for excellence.* Edinburgh: Scottish Executive.

Curtis, A (1998) *A curriculum for the pre-school child: learning to learn.* London: Routledge

Dahlberg, G, Moss, P and Pence, A (1999) *Beyond quality in early childhood education and care.* Lewes: Falmer Press.

Daily Telegraph (2009) Boys develop closer bonds with Bob the Builder than with parents. 25 May, p.8.

Daniel, P and Ivatts, J (1998) *Children and social policy.* Basingstoke: Macmillan.

Davis, H and Bourhill, M (2004) 'Crisis': the demonization of children and young people, in Scraton, P (ed) *'Crisis' in 'childhood'?* Abingdon: Routledge.

Daycare Trust (2008) *Childcare costs survey.* Available at **www.daycaretrust.org.uk/data/files/Research/costs_surveys/cost_survey2008.pdf**

De Beauvoir, S (1973) *The second sex.* New York: Vintage.

Department for Children, Education, Lifelong Learning and Skills (DCELLS) (2008) *Framework for children's learning for 3 to 7 year olds in Wales.* Cardiff: Welsh Assembly Government.

Department for Children, Schools and Families (DCSF) (2007) *The children's plan: building better futures.* London: DCSF.

Department for Children, Schools and Families (DCSF) (2008) *Graduate leader fund: further information on purpose and implementation.* Available online at **www.dcsf.gov.uk/everychildmatters/_search/?s_Keywords=graduate+leader+fund%3A+further+information+on+purpose+and+implementation**

Department for Children, Schools and Families (DCSF) (2009) *Child poverty strategy.* Available online at **www.dcsf.gov.uk/everychildmatters/strategy/parents/childpoverty/strategy/cpstrategy/**

Department for Education and Employment/School Curriculum and Assessment Authority (DfEE/SCAA) (1996) *Desirable outcomes for children's learning on entering compulsory education.* London: DfEE/SCAA.

Department for Education and Employment (DfEE)(2000) *Curriculum guidance for the Foundation Stage.* London: Qualifications and Curriculum Authority.

Department for Education and Science (DES) (1978) *Report of the committee of inquiry into the education of handicapped children and young people (The Warnock Report).* London: HMSO.

Department for Education and Skills (DfES) (2001) *Code of practice for children with special educational needs.* London: DfES.

Department for Education and Skills (DfES) (2002) *Birth to three matters.* London: DfES.

Department for Education and Skills (DfES) (2003) *Every child matters (Green Paper).* London: HMSO

Department for Education and Skills (DfES) (2004a) *Every child matters: change for children.* London: DfES.

Department for Education and Skills (DfES) (2004b) *The Children Act.* London: HMSO.

Department for Education and Skills (DfES) (2005) *Children's workforce strategy.* Available online from **www.dcsf.gov.uk/consultations/downloadableDocs/5958-DfES-ECM.pdf**

Department for Education and Skills (DfES) (2007) *Early Years Foundation Stage.* London: DfES.

Department for Transport (DfT) (2007) *National travel survey 2006.* London: Transport Statistics.

Department of Health (DoH) (1989) *The Children Act.* London: HMSO.

Department of Health (DoH) (2004) *National service framework for children, young people and maternity services.* London: Department of Health.

Department of Health (DoH) (2008) *Child health promotion programme.* London: HMSO.

Department for Work and Pensions (DWP) (2003) *UK action plan on social inclusion 2003–2005.* London: Department for Work and Pensions.

Derman-Sparks, L (1989) *The anti-bias curriculum.* Washington, DC: National Association for the Education of Young Children.

Dobash, RE and Dobash, R (1992) *Women, violence and social change.* London: Routledge.

Donnelly, P (2007) The Republic of Ireland, in Clark, MM and Waller, T (eds) *Early education and care: policy and practice.* London: Sage.

Dowling, M (1992) *Education 3–5.* 2nd edition. London: Paul Chapman Publishing.

Esping-Anderson, G (1989) *The three worlds of welfare capitalism.* Cambridge: Polity Press.

Esping-Anderson, G (ed) (1996) *Welfare states in transition.* London: Sage.

Farrell, A (ed) (2005) *Ethical research with children.* Maidenhead: Open University Press/McGraw-Hill Education.

Foley, P (2001) The development of child health and welfare services in England (1900–1948), in Foley, P, Roche, J and Tucker, S (eds) *Children in society: contemporary theory, policy and practice.* Basingstoke: Palgrave.

Foley, P (2008a) Listening across generations, in Foley, P and Leverett, S (eds) *Connecting with children: developing working relationships.* Bristol: The Policy Press.

Foley, P (2008b) Reflecting on skills for work with children, in Foley, P and Rixon, A (eds) *Changing Children's Services: working and learning together.* Bristol: The Policy Press.

Foley, P, Roche, J and Tucker, S (eds)(2001) *Children in society: contemporary theory, policy and practice.* Basingstoke: Palgrave.

Foucault, M (1977) *Discipline and punish.* London: Allen Lane.

Franklin, B (ed) (2002) *The new handbook of children's rights: comparative policy and practice.* Abingdon: Routledge.

Freeman, C, Henderson, P and Kettle, J (1999) *Planning with children for better communities: the challenge to professionals.* Bristol: The Policy Press.

Frønes, I (1994) Dimensions of childhood, in Qvortrup, J, Sgritta, G and Wintersberger, G (eds) *Childhood matters: social theory, practice and politics.* Aldershot: Avebury.

Furedi, F (2001) *Paranoid parenting: abandon your anxieties and be a good parent.* London: Allen Lane.

Future Foundation (2006) *The changing face of parenting.* London: Future Foundation.

Gabriel, N (2007) Being a child today, in Willan, J, Parker Rees, R and Savage, J (eds) *Early childhood studies.* 2nd edition. Exeter: Learning Matters.

Gabriel, N (2010) Adults' concepts of childhood, in Parker, Rees, R, Leeson, C, Willan, J and Savage, J (eds) *Early childhood studies.* 3rd edition. Exeter: Learning Matters.

Giddens, A (1984) *The constitution of society: outline of a theory of structuration.* Cambridge: Polity Press.

Giddens, A (1998) *The third way: the renewal of social democracy.* Cambridge: Polity Press.

Gill, T (2007) *No Fear: Growing up in a risk-averse society.* London: Gulbenkian Foundation.

Gittens, D (1998) *The child in question.* Basingstoke: Macmillan Press.

Goldson, B (2001) The demonization of children: from the symbolic to the institutional, in Foley, P, Roche, J and Tucker, S (eds) *Children in society: contemporary theory, policy and practice.* Basingstoke: Palgrave.

Goldstein, DM (1998) Nothing bad intended: child discipline, punishment and survival in a shantytown in Rio de Janeiro, Brazil, in Montgomery, H, Burr, R and Woodhead, M (eds) *Changing childhoods, local and global.* Buckingham: Open University Press.

Guldberg, H (2009) *Reclaiming childhood: freedom and play in an age of fear.* Abingdon: Routledge.

Handley, G (2009) Children's rights to participation, in Waller, T (ed) *An introduction to early childhood: a multidisciplinary approach.* 2nd edition. London: Paul Chapman Publishing.

Hardman, C (1973) Can there be an anthropology of children? *Journal of the Anthropological Society of Oxford.* 4(1): 85–99.

Harms, T, Clifford M and Cryer, C (1998) *Early childhood environment rating scale, revised edition (ECERS-R).* Williston, VT: Teachers College Press.

Hart, R (1992) *Children's participation from tokenism to citizenship.* Florence: UNICEF Innocenti Research Centre.

Hendrick, H (1994) *Child welfare: 1870-1989.* London: Routledge.

Hendrick, H (1997a) Constructions and reconstructions of British childhood: an interpretive survey, 1800 to the present, in James, A and Prout, A (eds) *constructing and reconstructing childhood: contemporary issues in the sociological study of childhood.* 2nd edition. London: Falmer Press.

Hendrick, H (1997b) *Children, childhood and English society 1880-1990.* Cambridge: Cambridge University Press.

Hendrick, H (ed)(2005) *Child welfare and social policy.* Bristol: The Policy Press.

HM Treasury (2004) *Choice for parents, the best start for children: a ten-year strategy for childcare.* London: HMSO.

Hevey, D (2009) Professional work in early childhood, in Waller, T (ed) *An introduction to early childhood.* 2nd edition. London: Sage.

Hill, M and Tisdall, K (1997) *Children and society.* Harlow: Pearson Education.

Hohman, U (2010) Recent developments in the Early Years workforce: insights from Germany, in Parker Rees, R, Leeson, C, Willan, J and Savage, J (eds) *Early childhood studies.* 3rd edition. Exeter: Learning Matters.

Holloway, S and Valentine, G (2000) (eds) *Children's geographies: living, playing, learning.* Abingdon: Routledge.

Holt, J (1975) *Escape from childhood; the needs and rights of children.* London: Penguin.

Hood, S (2001) *The state of London's children.* London: Office of the Children's Rights Commissioner for London.

Horn, P (1989) *The Victorian and Edwardian schoolchild.* Gloucester: Alan Sutton Publishing.

Hutchby, I and Moran Ellis, J (eds) (1998) *Children and social competence: arenas of action.* Lewes: Falmer Press.

Hutchby, I and Moran Ellis, J (eds) (2001) *Children, technology and culture: the impact of technologies in children's everyday lives.* Abingdon: RoutledgeFalmer.

International Labour Organisation (ILO) (2006) *The end of child labour: within reach.* Geneva: ILO, available online at **www.ilo.org/public/english/standards/relm/ilc/ilc95/pdf/rep-i-b.pdf**.

Jackson, S and Fawcett, M (2009) Early childhood policy and services, in Maynard, T and Thomas, N (eds) *An introduction to early childhood studies.* 2nd edition. London: Sage.

James, A and James, A (2004) *Constructing childhood: theory, policy and social practice.* Abingdon: Palgrave Macmillan.

James, A and James, A (2008) *Key concepts in childhood studies.* London: Sage.

James, A and Prout, A (eds) (1997) *Constructing and reconstructing childhood: contemporary issues in the sociological study of childhood.* Abingdon: Falmer Press.

James, A, Jenks, C and Prout, A (2001) *Theorizing childhood.* Cambridge: Polity Press.

Jenks, C (1995) Watching your step: the history and practice of the flaneur, in Jenks C. (ed) *Visual Culture.* London: Routledge.

Jenks, C (1996) *Childhood.* London: Routledge.

John, M (2003) *Children's rights and power: charging up for the new century.* London: Jessica Kingsley.

Jones, C and Leverett, S (2008) Policy into practice: assessment, evaluation and multi-agency working with children, in Foley, P and Rixon, A (eds) *Changing children's services: working and learning together.* Bristol: The Policy Press.

Kaldor, M (1999) *New and old wars: organised violence in a global era.* Cambridge: Polity Press.

Karpf, A (2003) For what it's worth. *Guardian,* 1 January, p.7.

Katz, C (2005) The terrors of hypervigilance: security and the compromised spaces of contemporary childhood, in Qvortrup, J (ed) *Studies in modern childhood: society, agency, culture.* Basingstoke: Palgrave Macmillan.

Katz, J (1997) *Virtuous reality: how America surrendered discussion of moral values to opportunists, nitwits and blockheads like William Bennett.* New York: Random House.

Katz. LG (1993) Multiple perspectives on the quality of early childhood programmes. *European Early Childhood Education Research Journal.* 1(2): 5–9.

Kehily, MJ and Montgomery, H (2004) Innocence and experience: a historical approach to childhood and sexuality, in Kehily, MJ (ed) *An introduction to childhood studies.* Maidenhead: Open University Press/ McGraw-Hill Education.

Kettle, J (2008) Children's experience of community regeneration, in Jones, P, Moss, D, Tomlinson, P and Welch, S (eds) (2007) *Childhood: services and provision for children.* Harlow: Pearson Longman.

Lahman, MKE (2008) Always othered: ethical research with children. *Journal of Early Childhood Research,* 6(3): 281–300.

Laming, Lord (2003) *The Victoria Climbié Inquiry report.* London: The Stationery Office.

Lancaster, YP (2006) Listening to young children: respecting the voice of the child, in Pugh, G and Duffy, B (eds) *Contemporary issues in the early years.* 4th edition. London: Sage.

Lancaster, YP (2010) Listening to young children: Enabling children to be seen and heard, in Pugh, G and Duffy, B (eds) *Contemporary issues in the Early Years.* 5th edition. London: Sage.

Lancaster, YP and Broadbent, V (2003) *Listening to young children.* Maidenhead: Open University Press/ McGraw-Hill Education.

Lansdown, G (2005) *The evolving capacities of the child.* Florence: UNICEF Innocenti Research Centre.

Layard, R and Dunn, J (2009) *A good childhood: searching for values in a competitive age.* London: Penguin Books.

Leach, P (1994) *Children first.* London: Michael Joseph.

Learner, S (2009) Streets are 'no go' areas for children playing. *Nursery World,* 19 August, p.3.

Lee, N (2001a) *Childhood and society: growing up in an age of uncertainty.* Buckingham: Open University Press.

Lee, N (2001b) The extensions of childhood, in Hutchby, I and Moran Ellis, J (eds) *Children, technology and culture: the impact of technologies in children's everyday lives.* Abingdon: Routledge Falmer.

Leverett, S (2008a) Parenting: politics and concepts for practice, in Foley, P and Rixon, A (eds) *Changing children's services: working and learning together.* Bristol: The Policy Press.

Leverett, S (2008b) Children's participation, in Foley, P and Leverett, S (eds) *Connecting with children: developing working relationships.* Bristol: The Policy Press.

Lewis, J (1986) Anxieties about the family and relationships between parents, children and the state in twentieth century England, in Richard, M and Light, P (eds) *Children of social worlds.* Cambridge: Polity Press.

Locke, J (1692) *Some thoughts concerning education.* Full text available online at **www.fordham.edu/halsallmod/ 1692locke-education.html**

Louv, R (2008) *Last child in the woods: saving our children from nature-deficit disorder.* Chapel Hill, NY: Algonquin Books.

Mac Naughton, G (2003) *Shaping early childhood: learners, curriculum and contexts.* Maidenhead: Open University Press/ McGraw-Hill Education.

Malaguzzi, L (1996) *The hundred languages of children.* Reggio Emilia: Reggio Children.

Marsh, J (2002) Electronic toys: why should we be concerned? A response to Levin and Rosenquest. *Contemporary Issues in Early Childhood*, 3(1):132–8.

Marsh, J (ed) (2005) *Popular culture, new media and digital literacy in early childhood.* Abingdon: Routledge Falmer.

Matthews, H (2002) Children and regeneration: setting the agenda for community participation and integration. *Children and Society,* 17: 264–76.

Mayall, B (2002) *Towards a sociology of childhood: thinking from children's lives.* Buckingham: Open University Press.

McDowall Clark, R and Hanson, K (2007) The Early Years network: a case study in continuing professional development. *Journal of the European Teacher Education Network (JETEN)*, 3: 13–21.

McDowall Clark, R and Baylis, S (2010) The new professionals: leading for change, in Reed, M and Canning, N (eds) *Reflective Practice in the Early Years.* London: Sage.

Midgely, C (2006) Our cotton wool kids. *Times*, 19 July. Available online at **http://women.timesonline.co.uk/tol/ life_and_style/women/families/article689316.ece.**

Morgan, D (1996) *Family connections: an introduction to family studies.* Cambridge: Polity Press.

Moss, P (2009) *Early childhood education and care: dangers, possibilities and choices.* Paper given at the Norwegian Centre for Child Research (NOSEB) Conference, Trondheim, Norway, 29–30 April.

Moss, P and Penn, H (1996) *Transforming nursery education.* London: Paul Chapman Publishing.

Moss, P and Petrie, P (2002) *From children's services to children's spaces; public policy, children and childhood.* Abingdon: Routledge.

Munton, AG, Mooney, A and Rowland, L (1995) Deconstructing quality: a conceptual framework for the new paradigm in day care provision for the under eights. *Early Child Development and Care.* 114: 11–23.

Murdock, G (1968) The universality of the nuclear family, in Bell, N and Vogel, E (eds) *A modern introduction to the family.* New York: Free Press.

National Evaluation of Sure Start (NESS) (2004) *Towards understanding Sure Start local programmes: summary of findings from the national evaluation.* Nottingham: DfES.

National Evaluation of Sure Start (NESS) (2007) *National evaluation report: understanding variations in effectiveness amongst Sure Start local programmes.* Nottingham: DfES.

Nimmo, J (2008) Young children's access to real-life: an examination of the growing boundaries between children in childcare and adults in the community. *Contemporary Issues in Early Childhood.* Vol 9 (1): 3–13.

Nutbrown, C and Clough, P (2006) *Inclusion in the Early Years: critical analyses and enlightened narratives.* London: Sage.

Oakley, A (1994) Women and children first and last: parallels and differences between children's and women's studies, in Mayall, B (ed) *Children's childhoods: observed and experienced.* Lewes: Falmer.

Palmer, S (2006) *Toxic childhood: how the modern world is damaging ourchildren and what we can do about it.* London: Orion.

Papert, S (1993) *The children's machine: re-thinking school in the age of the computer.* New York: Basic Books.

Pascal, C and Bertram, T (1997) *Effective early learning: case studies in improvement.* London: Hodder & Stoughton.

Penn, H. (2004) *Unequal childhoods: young children's lives in poor countries.* Abingdon: Routledge.

Penn, H. (2005) *Understanding early childhood: issues and controversies.* Maidenhead: Open University Press/McGraw-Hill Education**.**

Penn, H (2007) Childcare market management: how the United Kingdom government has reshaped its role in developing early childhood education and care. *Contemporary Issues in Early Childhood,* 8(3): 192–207.

Pollock, L (1983) *Forgotten children: parent–child relations from 1500–1900.* Cambridge: Cambridge University Press.

Postman, N (1987) A*musing ourselves to death.* London: Methuen.

Postman, N (1994) *The disappearance of childhood.* London: WH Allen.

Pound, L, Pramling-Samulesson, I and Fleer, M (eds) (2009) *Play and learning in early childhood settings: international perspectives.* Dordrecht: Springer.

Prensky, M (2001) Digital natives, digital immigrants. *On the Horizon.* 9(5): 1–6.

Prout, A (2000) Children's participation: control and self-regulation in British late modernity. *Children and Society.* 14(4): 304–15.

Prout, A (2005) *The future of childhood.* Abingdon: Routledge Falmer.

Prout, A and James, A (1997) A new paradigm for the sociology of childhood? Provenance, promise and problems, in James, A and Prout, A (eds) *Constructing and reconstructing childhood: contemporary issues in the sociological study of childhood.* 2nd edition. London: Routledge Falmer.

Pugh, G (2010) The policy agenda for early childhood services, in Pugh, G and Duffy, B (eds) *Contemporary Issues in the Early Years.* 5th edition. London: Sage.

Pugh, G and Duffy, B (eds) (2010) *Contemporary issues in the Early Years*. 5th edition. London: Sage.

Qualifications and Curriculum Authority/Department for Education and Employment (QCA/DfEE) (2000) *Curriculum guidance for the Foundation Stage.* London: QCA and DfEE.

Qureshi, H (2009) New female breadwinners. *Guardian*, 24 October, p.1.

Qvortrup, J, (1994) Childhood matters: an introduction, in Qvortup, J Bardy, M, Sgritta, G and Wintersberger, H (eds) (1994) *Childhood matters: social theory, practice and politics.* Aldershot: Avebury.

Rasmussen, K (2004) Places for children – children's places. *Childhood*, 11: 155–73.

Reed, M (2009) *A picture of Early Years practice relating to diversity in policy and curriculum practice in the four nations of the United Kingdom.* Paper delivered at the European Early Childhood Education Research Association (EECERA) Conference in Strasbourg, France 26–29 August.

Robb, M (2001) The changing experience of childhood, in Foley, P, Roche, J and Tucker, S (eds) *Children in society: contemporary theory, policy and practice.* Basingstoke: Palgrave.

Roberts, H (2008) Listening to children: and hearing them, in Christenson, P and James, A (eds) *Research with children.* 2nd edition. London: Falmer Press.

Roberts-Holmes, G (2009) Inclusive policy and practice, in Maynard, T and Thomas, N (eds) *An introduction to early childhood studies.* 2nd edition. London: Sage.

Rogoff, B (2003) *The cultural nature of human development.* Oxford: Oxford University Press.

RoSPA (Royal Society for the Prevention of Accidents) (2007) *Review 06:07.* Birmingham: RoSPA.

Rousseau, JJ (1974) *Emile.* London: Dent.

Rutter, M (1981) *Maternal deprivation reassessed.* 2nd edition. London: Penguin Books.

Sanders, B (2009) Interagency and multidisciplinary working, in Maynard, T and Thomas, N (eds) *An introduction to early childhood studies*. 2nd edition. London: Sage.

Scraton, P (2004) (ed) *'Childhood' in 'crisis'?* Abingdon: Routledge.

Silva, EB and Smart, C (1999) *The new family.* London: Sage.

Siraj-Blatchford, I and Yeok-Lin, Wong (1999) Defining and evaluating quality early childhood education in an international context: dilemmas and possibilities. *Early Years,* 20(1): 7–18.

Smart, C (1984) *The ties that bind.* London: Routledge and Kegan Paul.

Stone, B and Rixon, A (2008) Working together for children?, in Foley, P and Rixon, A (eds) *Changing children's services: working and learning together.* Bristol: The Policy Press.

Smith, F and Barker, J (2000) Contested spaces: children's experiences of out of school care in England and Wales. *Childhood.* 7: 315–33.

Social Exclusion Unit (SEU) (1998) *Bringing Britain together: a national strategy for neighbourhood renewal.* London: The Stationery Office.

Social Trends (2009) Available at **www.statistics.gov.uk/socialtrends39/**

Stonewall (2004) *The age of consent.* Available online at **www.stonewall.org.uk/at_home/hate_crime_ domestic_violence_and_criminal_law/2643.asp**

Sure Start (2002) *Birth to three matters: a framework to support children in their earliest years.* London: Sure Start Unit.

Sylva, K (2010) Quality in early childhood settings, in Sylva, K, Melhuish, EC, Sammons, P, Siraj-Blatchford, I and Taggart, B (eds) *Early childhood matters: evidence from the effective pre-school and primary education project.* Abingdon: Routledge.

Sylva, K, Melhuish, E, Sammons, P, Siraj-Blatchford, I and Taggart, B (2004) *The effective provision of pre-school education (EPPE) project: final report: effective pre-school education.* London: DfES and Institute of Education, University of London.

Sylva, K, Melhuish, E, Sammons, P, Siraj-Blatchford, I and Taggart, B (2010) *Early childhood matters: evidence from the effective pre-school and primary education project.* Abingdon: Routledge.

Sylva, K and Pugh, G (2005) Transforming the Early Years in England. *Oxford Review of Education.* 31(1): 11–27.

Sylva, K and Taylor, H (2006) Effective settings: evidence from research, in Pugh, G and Duffy, B (eds) *Contemporary issues in the Early Years.* 4th edition. London: Sage.

Tapscott, D (1998) *Growing up digital: the rise of the net generation.* New York: McGraw-Hill.

Taunton, M (2009) Ties that bound. *Times Literary Supplement,* no 5548, 31 July.

Thomas, G and Thompson, G (2004) *A child's place.* London: Demos/Green Alliance.

Tomlinson, P (2008) The politics of childhood, in Jones, P, Moss, D, Tomlinson, P and Welch, S (eds) *Childhood: Services and Provision for Children.* Harlow: Pearson Longman.

Tucker, N (1977) *What is a Child?* London: Fontana.

UNICEF (2002) *The State of the World's Children.* New York: UNICEF.

UNICEF (2006) *The State of the World's Children.* New York: UNICEF.

UNICEF (2007) *The State of the World's Children.* New York: UNICEF.

Valentine, G (2004) *Public space and the culture of childhood.* Aldershot: Ashgate.

Valentine, G (1996) Children should be seen and not heard: the production and transgression of adults' public space. *Urban Geography,* 17: 205–20.

Viruru, R (2008) Childhood labour in India: issues and complexities. *Contemporary Issues in Early Childhood,* 9(3): 224–33.

Wagg, S (1992) I blame the parents: childhood and politics in modern Britain. *Sociology Review,* 1(4): 10–15.

Walker, G (2008) Safeguarding children: visions and values, in Jones, P, Moss, D, Tomlinson, P and Welch, S (eds) *Childhood: services and provision for children*. Harlow: Pearson Longman.

Waller, T (eds) (2009) *An introduction to early childhood: a multidisciplinary approach*. 2nd edition. London: Sage.

Wells, K (2009) *Childhood in a global perspective*. Cambridge: Polity Press.

Whalley, M and the Pen Green Team (2008) *Involving parents in their children's learning*. 2nd edition. London: Paul Chapman Publishing.

Williams, F (1989) *Social policy: a critical introduction*. Cambridge: Polity Press.

Woodhead, M (1998) 'Quality' in early childhood programmes – a contextually appropriate approach. *International Journal of Early Years Education*, 6(1): 5–17.

Woodhead, M (2009) *The 'modern child' in global contexts: insights from the Young Lives Project*. Paper delivered at the Norwegian Centre for Child Research (NOSEB) Conference, Trondheim, Norway, 29–30 April.

Wyn Siencen, S and Thomas, S (2007), in Clark, MM and Waller, T (eds) *Early education and care: policy and practice*. London: Sage.

Wyness, M (2006) *Childhood and society: an introduction to the sociology of childhood*. Basingstoke: Palgrave.

Zelizer, V (1994) *Pricing the priceless child: the changing social value of children*. Princeton NJ: Princeton University Press.

Index

Added to a page number 'f' denotes a figure.